Celebrate with Books

Celebrate with Books

Booktalks for Holidays and Other Occasions

Rosanne J. Blass

A Member of the Greenwood Publishing Group

Westport, Connecticut • London

Library of Congress Cataloging-in-Publication Data

Blass, Rosanne J., 1937-
  Celebrate with books : booktalks for holidays and other occasions / Rosanne J. Blass.
    p. cm.
  Includes bibliographical references and index.
  ISBN 1-59158-076-5 (alk. paper)
  1. Children—Books and reading—Bibliography. 2. Holidays—Bibliography.
  3. Children's libraries—Activity programs. 4. Book talks. I. Title.
  Z1037.A1B58234 2005
  028.1'62—dc22   2005018015

British Library Cataloguing in Publication Data is available.

Copyright © 2005 by Libraries Unlimited

All rights reserved. No portion of this book may be
reproduced, by any process or technique, without the
express written consent of the publisher.

Library of Congress Catalog Card Number: 2005018015
ISBN: 1–59158–076–5

First published in 2005

Libraries Unlimited, 88 Post Road West, Westport, CT 06881
A Member of the Greenwood Publishing Group, Inc.
www.lu.com

Printed in the United States of America

The paper used in this book complies with the
Permanent Paper Standard issued by the National
Information Standards Organization (Z39.48–1984).

10 9 8 7 6 5 4 3 2 1

Contents

	Acknowledgment and Dedication ix	
	Introduction xi	
Chapter 1:	Holidays in General 1	
	1.1. Cultures Around the World 2	
	1.2. African-American 4	
	1.3. Asian 5	
	1.4. Indian 6	
	1.5. Islamic 12	
	1.6. Jewish 13	
	1.7. Spanish 16	
	1.8. North American 19	
Chapter 2:	January 21	
	2.1. Martin Luther King Jr. Day 23	
	2.2. Ramadan and Id-ul-Fitr 27	
Chapter 3:	February 33	
	3.1. National African-American History Month 35	
	3.2. Groundhog Day 39	
	3.3. Chinese New Year 42	
	3.4. Valentine's Day 44	
	3.5. Presidents' Day 47	
Chapter 4:	March 53	
	4.1. National Women's History Month 55	

	4.2. Mardi Gras and Carnival ... 59
	4.3. St. Patrick's Day ... 62
	4.4. Holi ... 66
Chapter 5:	April ... 69
	5.1. National Poetry Month ... 71
	5.2. Passover ... 74
	5.3. Easter ... 77
	5.4. Earth Day ... 81
Chapter 6:	May ... 85
	6.1. National Asian/Pacific Heritage Month ... 87
	6.2. Cinco de Mayo ... 92
	6.3. Mother's Day ... 94
Chapter 7:	June ... 99
	7.1. Flag Day ... 100
	7.2. Father's Day ... 102
	7.3. Juneteenth ... 106
Chapter 8:	July ... 109
	8.1. Canada Day ... 110
	8.2. Independence Day ... 111
	8.3. Pioneer Day (Mormon) ... 114
Chapter 9:	August ... 117
	9.1. Back to School ... 118
Chapter 10:	September ... 123
	10.1. National Hispanic Heritage Month ... 125
	10.2. Labor Day ... 128
	10.3. Grandparents' Day ... 131
	10.4. Rosh Hashanah ... 135

Contents ■ vii

Chapter 11: October 139
        11.1. Diversity Awareness Month 140
        11.2. Columbus Day 144
        11.3. Diwali. 146
        11.4. Day of the Dead 148
        11.5. Halloween 151

Chapter 12: November 155
        12.1. National American Indian Heritage Month 157
        12.2. Election Day 161
        12.3. Veterans' Day 164
        12.4. Thanksgiving 168

Chapter 13: December 173
        13.1. Pearl Harbor Day 174
        13.2. Hanukkah. 177
        13.3. Christmas. 181
        13.4. Kwanzaa. 185

Chapter 14: Other Occasions 191
        14.1. Birthdays 192
        14.2. Loose Teeth and the Tooth Fairy 196
        14.3. New Siblings 201

        Index 207

Acknowledgment and Dedication

I wish to thank my editor, Barbara Ittner, for shepherding this book from start to finish, always pushing me to a higher standard. Thanks for the learning and growth you've provided to me and for the quality book that you've enabled me to produce!

This book is dedicated to the children's librarians, media specialists, and others who open the world of books to young readers in memory of Verlie Gherkin, children's librarian at the North Branch Public Library, Minneapolis, Minnesota. It was she who opened the world of books to me. Beginning with story hour while I was a preschooler, Miss Gherkin became an important person in my life. She guided me through my elementary and high school years—always with another book for me tucked away at her desk. She then supported me as a teacher education student by helping me find appropriate books to use with my teacher education courses and as a beginning teacher by providing me with bags of books for my sixth graders.

Hopefully, this book will be an aid to those who now open the world of books to today's young readers.

Introduction

Celebrating with Books invites you to open the world of books and the power of literacy to children. The world of books enables readers to explore, define, and redefine themselves (who they are, who and what they might become) and their world (as it is and might be). It enables readers to develop intellectually, aesthetically, and spiritually; to lead more thoughtful lives; and to participate more fully in the richness of all creation.

The power of literacy becomes a tool for personal and social change, a tool with which to explore questions, develop understandings, and freely share ideas and information. It develops as a social process—interactive and constructive—between the reader, the text, and others. In particular, conversation and discussion based on the text raise questions and increase motivation to read more. Adults, who share their passion for books with children and encourage children to respond, instill that passion in their young audience. Booktalks with and for young readers is one vehicle for sharing the passion.

Celebrating with Books is a collection of holiday Booktalks for elementary and middle school–age children (K–6) organized according to the calendar year. Holidays and other observances such as National African-American History Month, National Women's History Month, and others have been identified for each month. Holidays of world cultures such as the Hindu festivals of Holi and Diwali and other cultures are also included. Because many children's books about the holidays of world cultures tend to be collections rather than individual books, they are organized by culture and are treated in the first chapter, "Holidays in General." For example, "Holidays in General" includes books about cultures around the world, Asian cultures, Islamic culture, and others. The last chapter, "Other Occasions," addresses special events that occur throughout the year, such as birthdays, loose teeth and the tooth fairy, and new siblings.

One hundred seventy-one newly published (2000–2004) fiction and nonfiction books by award-winning authors and illustrators, books that reflect emerging trends, and books that reflect an appreciation of diversity were selected for inclusion. Publications such as *Booklist, Book Report, Book Talk, Bulletin of the Center for Children's Books, JOYS, School Library Journal, VOYA—Voices of Youth Advocates,* and *Wilson Bulletin* were consulted for reviews and recommendations. In order to provide balance and diversity, some books published in the 1990s were included, but emphasis was on new releases. The wide assortment of books selected for inclusion will appeal to a wide range of readers in the elementary and middle grades—picture books, alphabet books, concept books, early readers, easy chapter books, novellas, junior novels, photo-essays, biographies, poetry, and humor.

Each entry provides bibliographic information, recommended age level, a book summary, a Booktalk, Learning Extensions with identification of appropriate areas of the curriculum, and related books for further reading. Age levels are generally based on publisher's recommendations with some modifications based on ease or difficulty of language used and concepts developed. Librarians, parents, and educators are urged to use these levels only as a general guide and to use their own judgment in selecting titles. Learning Extensions are intended to stimulate ideas rather than to give full, detailed activity directions. Librarians, parents, and educators will need to adapt these ideas to fit the needs of the children with whom they are working.

The primary audiences for this book are children's librarians, school librarians, media specialists, and church and synagogue librarians who work with elementary and middle-grade (K–6) children. However, parents, especially those who homeschool, and teachers will also find the books useful. Public librarians who serve young students in the library or who make school visits can use these Booktalks to promote their collection and services. School library media specialists and church and synagogue librarians will find the Booktalks valuable in selecting and promoting books in classrooms, in the media center, and in church and synagogue programs. They may also want to refer to this book when making selections for purchase. Classroom and reading teachers, curriculum specialists, church educators, and homeschool parents and teachers might use the book as a guide to identifying books for read-alouds or to identify books that complement specific topics they are covering in class.

TIPS AND GUIDELINES

Booktalks are a social approach to literacy development. Someone chooses and shares books with others. In this case, it is the adult who chooses and shares books with young readers. Be sure to read the books you choose before sharing them with children. Select only those books that you really like, love, or can be enthusiastic about. It is your love for the books that will light the spark of interest and curiosity that will motivate your audience to read the books. Feel free to modify and adapt your books to fit your own style and purposes. Take advantage of and maximize opportunities to encourage your young readers to revisit the book. The research base strongly supports the power of re-readings to strengthen and develop fluency, comprehension, and higher-level thinking skills.

Learning Extensions are natural rather than artificial extensions of the book, meaning that they are directly related to and flow from the book. They are intended to relate to the curriculum, such as social studies, language arts, and other areas, in order to connect reading to all school studies. Learning Extensions are designed to stimulate language, literacy, and cognitive development through oral language use, conversations, and discussions; through art, music, and drama; through inquiry, research, and critical thinking; and finally through service learning, character education, and values education activities.

CHILDREN'S LITERATURE TODAY

The books chosen for inclusion reflect emerging trends in publishing and an appreciation for diversity. The celebration of America, patriotism, and anniversaries; the influence of current events and technology; exciting illustrations; the continued popularity of series books; and the growing number of nonfiction documentaries and photo-essays are only a few of today's current trends.

Since 9/11, there has been an increase in books that celebrate America and patriotism, such as Louise Borden, *America Is ...;* Lynne Cheney, *America: A Patriotic Primer;* and Charles M. Schultz, *Peanuts: Here's to You America!* Books such as *The Bombing of Pearl Harbor in American History* by Anthony Nathan and Robert Gardner and *Navajo Code Talkers: America's Secret Weapon in World War II* by Nathan Aaseng mark the anniversaries of the bombing of Pearl Harbor and the end of World War II.

Judy Finchler's *Testing Miss Malarkey* and Doreen Cronin's *Duck for President* reflect the influence of current events, namely, the widespread emphasis on academic testing and an election year. The influence of technology can be seen in Lynne Cheney's *A Is for Abigail: An Almanac of American Women* and Peter Sis's *Madlenka*. Pages are busy with print, illustrations, and running text that borders pages and frames illustrations. The inclusion of music CDs, as in *Angel Face* by Sarah Weeks and *Grandma's Records* by Eric Velasquez, also reflects the increasing influence of technology.

Readers will find in these books some fine examples of outstanding illustrations, such as those in Brian Wildsmith's books *Exodus* and *The Easter Story,* Deborah Kogan Ray's *Hokusai: The Man Who Painted a Mountain,* and Russell Freedman's *Confucius: The Golden Rule.* Brian Wildsmith creates finely detailed illustrations illuminated with rich gold tones. The illustrations in *Hokusai: The Man Who Painted a Mountain* are authentic representations of Hokusai's paintings. The illustrations in *Confucius: The Golden Rule* are authentic representations of Chinese paintings.

Series books such as *Royal Diaries* and *My Name Is America* continue to be popular. Even Early Readers are appearing as series book, such as Claudia Mills's *Gus and Grandpa at Basketball* from the *Gus and Grandpa* series.

Nonfiction documentaries and photo-essays are appearing for both elementary and middle-grade students. Richard Watkins's *Slavery: Bondage Throughout History* and Catherine Clinton's *The Black Soldier: 1492 to the Present* retell the history of slavery and the history of the black soldier. Phillip Hoose's *It's Our World, Too! Young People Who Are Making a Difference* and *We Were There, Too!*

Young People in U.S. History recount the contributions of young people. Andrea Warren retells the stories of the children who traveled by train to new homes and families in the mid-west between 1910 and 1940 in *We Rode the Orphan Trains*. Finally, Patricia McMahon tells the story of dancers in wheelchairs.

The nonfiction documentaries and photo-essays about slavery, the black soldier, young people, orphans, and the disabled are just a small sampling of the growing number of new publications that foster awareness of and respect for diverse peoples and cultures. *Zoom* by Robert Munsch and *Moses Goes to a Concert* by Isaac Millman feature a spunky little girl in a wheelchair and a hearing-impaired boy and his friends. The *Royal Diaries* series and three books (*Wings and Rockets: The Story of Women in Air and Space* by Jeannine Atkins; *A Is for Abigail: An Almanac of American Women* by Lynne Cheney; and *The Sky's the Limit: Stories of Discovery by Women and Girls* by Catherine Thimmesh) recognize and celebrate the accomplishments of women. Two books of poetry, *A Humble Life: Plain Poems* by Linda Oatman High and *The Flag of Childhood: Poems from the Middle East* by Naomi Shihab Nye, foster awareness of Amish and Mennonite people and people from Middle Eastern cultures.

A fresh smorgasbord of books awaits young readers. It is my hope that you will sample and enjoy the feast and then share your enthusiasm with the young people in your life.

Let the book be your guide and make it memorable!

1
Holidays in General

INTRODUCTION

How do holidays get started? How do we celebrate? Not everyone celebrates the same holidays, but celebrations are universal. People around the world remember and honor family, national, and religious events with celebrations. Some books in this chapter introduce readers to cultures around the world and their holiday celebrations. Other books focus on the celebrations of specific cultures, such as African-American, Asian, Indian, Islamic, Jewish, North American, and Spanish cultures. Readers will learn more about their own holiday celebrations and discover new ones.

1.1 CULTURES AROUND THE WORLD

Introduce readers to Chinese, Hindu, Indian, Japanese, Latin/Hispanic, Vietnamese, African-American, Jewish, and North American holiday celebrations with the following books. Readers discover holidays such as the Chinese, Vietnamese, and Sikh celebrations of the New Year, the Hindu celebrations of Diwali and Holi, and the Japanese Hollyhock and Cherry Blossom Festivals and learn more about familiar holidays such as Valentine's Day and Mother's Day. Learning Extensions connect with art and social studies by having children draw pictures, locate countries on a world map, and make calendars that mark the dates of celebrations.

Chancellor, Deborah. *Holiday! Celebration Days Around the World.* New York: Dorling Kindersley Readers, 2000. 32p. $3.95. ISBN 0-7894-5711-3.

  PICTURE BOOK—Nonfiction
  Ages 5–8

Summary

Simple text and color photographs describe nine holidays: Chinese New Year, Valentine's Day, April Fool's Day, Mother's Day, Father's Day, Halloween, Diwali, Christmas, and Kwanzaa. The last page briefly describes six more holidays: Carnival, St. Patrick's Day, Hina Matsuri (Doll Festival), Holi, Easter, and Hanukkah.

Booktalk

How do holidays get started? How do we celebrate? We celebrate Valentine's Day in memory of St. Valentine, who signed a note to his jailer's daughter, "Love from your Valentine." Mother's Day began over 100 years ago when Anne Jarvis asked her friends to remember their mothers who had died by wearing white carnations to church. Diwali is a Hindu celebration of lights. You will find out about these and other holidays in *Holiday! Celebration Days Around the World.*

Learning Extensions (Art)

Select a holiday and draw pictures about how it is celebrated.

Robson, Pam. *How I Celebrate.* Brookfield, Conn.: Millbrook Press, 2000. 64p. $23.90. ISBN 0-7613-1952-2.

   📖 PICTURE BOOK—Nonfiction
      All Ages

Summary

Nine chapters introduce readers to family, national, and religious celebrations around the world. Included are a glossary and three calendars: one of celebrations around the world, another of National Days, and a third of Saints' Days.

Booktalk

Not everyone celebrates the same holidays you celebrate. For example, the New Year is celebrated around the world but at different times of the year: January, February, April, September, or even November, depending on the calendar that is used. Grace celebrates the New Year in January with party poppers and New Year's resolutions. In Times Square in New York City, a big shining ball drops from a flagpole at midnight. Chinese New Year is celebrated for two weeks, ending with the Lantern Festival. The Sikh New Year of Baisakhi is celebrated in April. For some children, tangerines bring good luck in the New Year. Who might those children be, and when do they celebrate?

Learning Extensions (Social Studies)

On a world map, find New York, Scotland, China, Vietnam, India, and Sydney, Australia. Make a calendar marking the dates that the New Year is celebrated in each country. Have children work in pairs to read about other celebrations and share the information.

Wilcox, Jane. *Why Do We Celebrate That?* London: Franklin Watts, 1996. 31p. $22.95. ISBN 0-531-14393-7.

   📖 PICTURE BOOK—Nonfiction
      All Ages

Summary

The origins of celebrations around the world are described accompanied by cartoonlike illustrations. Fifteen two-page spreads feature celebrations of life events, such as births and weddings, the seasons, holy days and people, and national holidays.

Booktalk

Select a celebration that is appropriate to the current season. For example, tell the children that spring is a beginning of new life celebrated with Purim and Passover, Good Friday, and Palm Sunday. Others celebrate the Indian festival of Shivrati, the Hindu festival of Holi, or the Japanese Hollyhock and Cherry Blossom Festivals. Many countries hold carnivals similar to Mardi Gras, held in New Orleans. How do you celebrate spring?

Learning Extensions (Art)

Make and illustrate calendars showing seasonal celebrations around the world. Serve a holiday or seasonal treat such as hot cross buns or Purim cookies. Have children share their calendars and illustrations with the group.

1.2 AFRICAN-AMERICAN

African-American holidays, such as Martin Luther King Jr.'s birthday, Black History Month, and Kwanzaa, and others that may not be as familiar, such as Juneteenth, Harambee, and Junkanoo, are presented. Children can conduct research, write reports about the holidays, and create clay sculptures that commemorate the holidays.

Winchester, Faith. *African-American Holidays*. Mankato, Minn.: Bridgestone Books, 1996. 23p. $18.60. ISBN 1-56065-456-2.

    PICTURE BOOK—Nonfiction; African-American
    Ages 7–12

Summary

Eight African-American holidays are presented using a two-page spread with a full-page photo and text for each of the following holidays: Martin Luther King Jr.'s Birthday, Black History Month, Malcolm X's Birthday, Juneteenth, Marcus Garvey's Birthday, Harambee,

Junkanoo, and Kwanzaa. A recipe for making clay sculptures, a pronunciation guide, words to know, suggested readings, addresses, and Internet sites complete the book.

Read-Aloud

Choose one of the holidays and read aloud the information.

Learning Extensions (research skills, language arts, and art).

Celebrate one of the holidays by having children use the suggested readings and Internet sites in the back of the book to research and write reports. Use the recipe in the back of the book to create clay sculptures that commemorate that holiday. Display the sculptures with the written reports.

1.3 ASIAN

Discover five celebrations from the Philippines: Ati-Atihan, Lent and Moriones, and festivals honoring San Isidro Labrador, Christmas, and rice festivals. Five Chinese festivals include Chinese New Year, the Lantern Festival, Qing Ming, the Dragon Boat Festival, and the Mid-Autumn Moon Festival. Japanese festivals include the honoring of girls and boys, the beginning of spring, the beginning of winter, and the Feast of Lanterns. Suggested responses related to language arts and art include retellings, dramatization, and learning a few Japanese words and phrases and the names for months.

Mendoza, Lunita. *Festivals of the World: Philippines.* Milwaukee, Wis.: Gareth Stevens, 1999. 32p. $24.67. ISBN 0-8368-2025-8.

 PICTURE BOOK—Nonfiction; Philippines
 Ages 7–12

Summary

Color photos and maps supplement the text, introducing readers to five celebrations: Ati-Atihan to honor the Christ Child; Lent and Moriones; festivals honoring San Isidro Labrador, the patron saint of farmers; Christmas; and rice festivals.

6 ■ *Holidays in General*

Booktalk

How many know where the Philippine islands are? (Use a world map or globe to locate the Philippines.) What holidays do children in the Philippines celebrate? *Festivals of the World: Philippines* tell us. Introduce the book by showing the cover while you read the title. Call attention to the maps on pages 4 to 5 to again locate the Philippines and identify the five celebrations that are featured in the book.

Learning Extensions (Language Arts, Art)

Divide the children into five small groups and have each small group retell how each of the five celebrations is observed. Use the directions in the book to make symbols, such as a parol that represents the star of Bethlehem. Serve a treat such as halo, a sweet dessert served at Christmas.

Simonds, Nina, Leslie Swartz, and The Children's Museum, Boston. *Moonbeams, Dumplings, & Dragon Boats: A Treasury of Chinese Holiday Tales, Activities & Recipes.* New York: Gulliver Books, 2002. 74p. Illustrated by Meilo So. $20.00. ISBN 0-15-201983-9.

 CHAPTER BOOK—Fiction; Activities; Crafts; Chinese
 Ages 8–12

Summary

Drawings and diagrams augment five Chinese festivals (Chinese New Year, the Lantern Festival, Qing Ming, the Dragon Boat Festival, and the Mid-Autumn Moon Festival) with stories, recipes, activities, and family traditions.

Booktalk

Introduce the book by showing the cover, reading the title, author, and illustrator. Select a story from the book to retell.

Extensions (Language Arts)

Block the story using the following format and embellish according to your comfort level.

Introduction	Hou Yi is a skilled archer with an enchanted bow.
	Hou Yi is in love with Chang E.
	Both want to live forever.
First Incident	Ten suns circled the Earth.
	One day all ten suns circled the Earth at the same time.
	The heat from the ten suns dried up all the rivers and flowers.
Second Incident	The Emperor commanded Hou Yi to save the people.
	Hou Yi destroyed nine suns by shooting them with his arrows.
	The Queen Mother of the Western Heavens rewarded Hou Yi by giving him the pill of immortality.
Third Incident	Hou Yi took the pill home, told Chang E, then hid the pill in the roof.
	Chang E found and swallowed the pill.
	Immediately Chang E began to float into the air.
Climax	Hou Yi came home, saw Chang E floating into the air, and knew that she had swallowed the pill.
	Hou Yi flew after Chang E.
	Chang E landed on the moon and was changed into a frog.
Ending	Chang E missed Hou Yi.
	Hou Yi missed Chang E.
	Once a month Hou Yi visits Chang E who becomes a beautiful princess.

Use a Chinese calendar to find the dates of the festival you will celebrate. Have the children use the directions on pages 70 to 71 to retell the story of Chang E and Hou Yi by writing a script, making puppets, and putting on a shadow puppet show. Use the recipe and directions and pages 68 to 69 to make and serve Rabbit-in-the-Moon Cookies.

Takabayashi, Mari. *I Live in Tokyo.* Boston: Houghton Mifflin, 2001. Unpaged. $16.00. ISBN 0-618-07702-2.

 📖 PICTURE BOOK—Fiction; Japanese
 Ages 5–10

Summary

Seven-year-old Mimiko takes readers through a year of her life in Tokyo. Organized by calendar months, each two-page spread introduces readers to holidays, foods, games, toys, family life, school, and celebrations in modern-day Japan. Delicate, detailed illustrations portray an authentic representation of Tokyo and Japanese culture, show how to wear a kimono, and give examples of the Chinese characters used in Japanese writing. The book ends with a listing of months of the year, a few words, numbers, and phrases in Japanese and English.

Booktalk

Have you ever heard of the Feast of Lanterns? Seven-year-old Mimiko lives in Tokyo, Japan. (Show picture of Mimiko.) Mimiko celebrates New Year's Day, Valentine's Day, and New Year's Eve. She also celebrates festivals honoring girls and boys, the beginning of spring, the beginning of winter, and the Feast of Lanterns. There are many other special festivals that Mimiko celebrates with balloons, masks, music, dancing, and games. Find out about Japanese holidays and how Mimiko celebrates them.

Learning Extensions (Language Arts)

Have children use information in the book to learn the Japanese names of the months, to count from 1 to 12 in Japanese, or to learn a few Japanese words or phrases.

1.4 INDIAN

India and South Asia are home to Hindu, Muslim, Sikh, and Buddhist cultures. Readers learn about the Hindu celebrations of Diwali, the Festival of Light, and Holi, the Festival of Bonfires, as well as celebrations of people in countries such as Sri Lanka, Nepal, Bhutan, and others. Selections offer opportunities to develop research, critical thinking, and map skills; to develop and present dramatizations; and to sample foods.

Hirst, Mike. *India.* Austin, Tex.: Raintree Steck-Vaughn, 1999. 32p. $25.64. ISBN 0-8172-5551-6.

 📖 PICTURE BOOK—Nonfiction; Hindu; Muslim; Sikh
 Ages 7–12

Summary

Four festivals of India—a Hindu wedding, the Muslim observance of Ramadan and Id-ul-Fitr, the Sikh celebration of Guru Nanak's birthday, and the Hindu celebration of Diwali, the Festival of Light—and their foods are presented. A recipe is included for each of the festivals. The book ends with a glossary and list of suggested resources.

Booktalk

Do you celebrate special occasions by eating special foods? Do your families prepare special foods to celebrate holidays? Introduce the book, calling attention to the foods shown on the cover. Tell the children that they will learn about the foods of India, such as grains, vegetables, and spices, and four festivals: a Hindu wedding, Ramadan and Id-ul-Fitr, Guru Nanak's Birthday, and Diwali. Show the children the inset showing where India is in the world.

Learning Extensions (Research Skills, Language Arts)

Divide children into four groups. Have each group select a festival from the book and do further research in the library or on the Internet. Using music, food, and props such as confetti, tiny oil lamps, or candles, have the children act out the festival they researched. Use the recipes in the book to treat the children to Barfi or Banana Lassi.

Kadodwala, Dilip, and Paul Gateshill. *Celebrate Hindu Festivals.* Crystal Lake, Ill.: Heinemann Library, 1997. 48p. $29.95. ISBN 0-431-06966-2.

 📖 PICTURE BOOK—Nonfiction; Hindu
 Ages 8–12

Summary

A brief description of Hinduism, the Hindu year, and a diagram of major religious festivals introduce a fuller explanation of the festivals and their celebrations.

Booktalk

Hindus are people who practice the religion of Hinduism, which had its beginnings in India. Hindus believe in one God, Brahman, who is in all things and takes the different forms of many different gods and goddesses. Hindus celebrate many different festivals to honor their many gods and goddesses and have many stories to tell about them. Diwali, the Festival of Lights; Holi, the Festival of Bonfires; and Ramnavami, a festival celebrating the birth of Rama, are only a few of the many festivals that Hindus celebrate. Learn more about the festivals and their celebrations in *Celebrate Hindu Festivals*.

Learning Extensions (Critical Thinking Skills, Language Arts)

Use the diagram on page 6 as guide to have the children make a chart of Hindu months, festivals, what the festivals celebrate, and the gods and goddesses who are honored with each festival.

Marchant, Kerena. *Hindu Festival Tales*. Austin, Tex.: Raintree Steck-Vaughn, 2001. 32p. Illustrated by Rebecca Gryspeerdt. $25.64. ISBN 0-7398-2734-0.

 PICTURE BOOK—Fiction; Hindu
 Ages 7–12

Summary

Traditional tales and poems, a song, and even a recipe for Hindu festivals are shared. Three stories celebrate Holi, the birth of Krishna, and Diwali. Two poems are used to celebrate a festival for brothers and sisters and a festival honoring the elephant-headed god of obstacles. A play celebrates the festival of good triumphing over evil, and a song honors Krishna and Rama. A recipe for sweets is included for the festival for brothers and sisters. The book concludes with information about Hindu festivals and a glossary.

Booktalk

Retell the story in the play on page 16.

Learning Extensions (Language Arts)

Assign roles to the children and have them reenact the play using the masks, props, sound effects, and music suggested in the book. If you have more than 10 children in your group, they can be the monkey and demon armies. Perform the play for friends and family.

Make invitations and programs to give to family and friends. Use the recipe for sweets on page 9 to make the refreshments.

Viesti, Joe, and Diane Hall. *Celebrate! In South Asia.* New York: Lothrop, Lee and Shepard Books, 1996. Unpaged. $15.89. ISBN 0-688-13775-X.

    PICTURE BOOK—Nonfiction
    Ages 7–12

Summary

Color photographs feature the holidays of Holi, a camel fair, Esala Perahera, Wesak, Baishakhi, Eid-ul-Fitr, Paro Tsechu, temple visits and offerings, and Tihar. A map at the back of the book shows the countries of India, Sri Lanka, Pakistan, Nepal, Bangladesh, Bhutan, and Myanmar (Burma).

Booktalk

You are going to meet people from seven different countries in South Asia as they celebrate different holidays. In India, people wear their worst clothes and throw powder and colored water on each other to celebrate Holi. What do you think of that! An elephant carries Buddha's tooth in a procession called Esala Perahera while lighted lanterns and lamps are used to celebrate Buddha's birth, enlightenment, and death. Then meet Bengali children celebrating their New Year, Muslim children celebrating the end of Ramadan, and Buddhists celebrating dance festivals. Finally, meet people in Burma lighting candles in their temples and children in Nepal decorating cows, dogs, and pets to celebrate their New Year.

Learning Extensions (Social Studies, Critical Thinking Skills, Language Arts)

Have the children find the countries of South Asia featured in this book (India, Sri Lanka, Pakistan, Nepal, Bangladesh, Bhutan, and Myanmar) on a world map. Then have them make a chart listing the countries, the names of the celebrations, what they are, and when they occur.

1.5 ISLAMIC

Learn about the development of Islamic culture, its beginnings in Arabia in the seventh century, and its founder, Muhammad. Two books explain the religion of Islam and its spread through Spain, Africa, Central Asia, Iran, India, China, and Southeast Asia and the festivals and ceremonies that Muslims observe.

Knight, Khadijah. *Celebrate Islamic Festivals.* Crystal Lake, Ill.: Heinemann Library, 1997. 48p. $29.93. ISBN 0-431-06964-6.

    PICTURE BOOK—Nonfiction; Muslim
Ages 7–12

Summary

Color photographs featuring Muslim children help introduce and explain the religion of Islam and the festivals celebrated throughout the year. A glossary and a listing of more books to read complete the book.

Booktalk

Hijrah, Ashura, Maulid, Laylat-ul-Isra wal Mi'raj, Laylat-ul-Barat, Ramadan, Laylat-ul-Qadr, Id-ul-Fitr, Hajj, and Id-ul-Ahha! What are these words? They are the names of Muslim festivals. How do Muslim children like 11-year-old Hussain and eight-year-old Fatima celebrate?

Learning Extensions (Critical Thinking Skills, Language Arts)

Discuss the festivals with the children, then prepare a chart listing What I Know and What I Want to Know. Invite Muslim children in your group or from your community to join you to tell more about their festivals and how they celebrate. Make and serve the recipe on page 27 as refreshments.

Wilkinson, Philip. *Islam.* New York: DK Publishing, 2002. 64p. $15.99. ISBN 0-7894-8871-X.

    PICTURE BOOK—Nonfiction
Ages 8–14

Summary

Color photographs along with the text present an overview of the Islam religion from its founding by Muhammad in Arabia in the seventh century and the basic tenets of its beliefs to its spread through Spain, Africa, Central Asia, Iran, India, China, and Southeast Asia. Eleven festivals and ceremonies are identified and described on pages 60 to 61.

Booktalk/Read-Aloud

Share the map on page 7, pointing out that Islam was founded in Arabia in the seventh century then spread to Africa, Central Asia, the Byzantine Empire, and on into Europe. Then turn to pages 60 to 61. Show the pictures and read aloud the introductory paragraph. Name the festivals and ceremonies that are shown.

Learning Extensions (Social Studies)

Create a world map showing the countries where Islam is practiced today.

1.6 JEWISH

Jewish history unfolds as the Jewish holidays (Rosh Hashanah, Yom Kippur, Hanukkah, Purim, Passover, Sukkot, Simchat Torah, Tu B'Shevat, Yom Ha-Shoah, Shabbat, and Shavuot) are observed throughout the year. Featured books include recipes, crafts, games, music, dance, and stories. Science, community service, critical thinking, music, dance, and discussion activities provide opportunities for children to celebrate the holidays.

Cooper, Ilene. *Jewish Holidays All Year Round.* New York: Harry N. Abrams, 2002. 80p. Illustrated by Elivia Savadier. $18.95. ISBN 0-8109-0550-7.

 📖 PICTURE BOOK—Nonfiction
  Ages 10–14

Summary

The foreword of this book invites readers to step into the Jewish Museum. The history of 12 Jewish holidays and how they are celebrated, pictures from the Jewish Museum, recipes, and directions for crafts and games complete the book.

Booktalk

How many of you are familiar with Rosh Hashanah, Yom Kippur, Hanukkah, Purim, and Passover? Give children an opportunity to respond. Do you know Sukkot, Simchat Torah, Tu B'Shevat, and Yom Ha-Shoah? They're all here in *Jewish Holidays All Year Round*.

Learning Extensions (Science, Community Service)

Follow the directions on page 47 to grow a sweet potato vine or parsley for Passover. Celebrate a holiday such as Tu B'Shevat, also known as the Jewish Arbor Day, by doing a spring cleanup on the school grounds. Plant trees, vines, shrubs, or even flowers. Serve fruits and nuts as a treat when finished.

See *Behold the Trees* in chapter 5 under "Earth Day." It tells how Israel was once covered with trees, reduced to a desert, and then restored to a fertile land with life-sustaining vegetation.

Goldin, Barbara. *Ten Holiday Jewish Children's Stories.* New York: Pitspopany Press, 2000. 41p. Illustrated by Jeffrey Allon. $16.95. ISBN 0-943706-47-5.

 📖 PICTURE BOOK—Folktales; Jewish
  Ages 6–9

Summary

An introductory chapter, "Jewish Storytelling," offers suggestions for enlivening stories for the holidays of Rosh Hashanah, Yom Kippur, Sukkot, Simchat Torah, Hanukkah, Tu B'Shevat, Purim, Passover, Shavuot, and Shabbat. Each story is followed by three questions to consider.

Booktalk/Read-Aloud

Select a story such as "Wake Up and Beat the Drums!" for Rosh Hashanah or "A King's Love" for Shavuot. Read aloud the italicized introduction about Nathan, Emily, and Grandma Sarah. Emphasize Grandma Sarah's last statement that the children must listen. Set the book aside and retell the story. After telling the story, conclude by reading the italicized ending of the story.

Learning Extensions (Critical Thinking Skills)

Engage the children in a discussion of the three questions that follow the story. Serve a treat appropriate to the holiday, such as honey and apples for Rosh Hashanah or blintzes for Shavuot.

Kimmelman, Leslie. *Dance, Sing, Remember: A Celebration of Jewish Holidays.* New York: HarperCollins, 2000. 34p. Illustrated by Ora Eitan. $18.95. ISBN 0-06-027725-4.

 📖 PICTURE BOOK—Nonfiction; Jewish
  Ages 4–8

Summary

Rosh Hashanah, Yom Kippur, Hanukkah, Purim, Passover, and seven other Jewish holidays (Sukkot, Simchat Torah, Tu B'Shevat, Yom Hashoah, Yom Ha'atzma'lit, Shavuot, and Shabbat) are included in this book. An illustrated two-page spread describes each holiday. Directions for games, food, recipes, music, and dance are included.

Booktalk

What do parsley, a dreidel, the hora, and a simple blessing have in common? They all play important parts in celebrating holidays. Perhaps you know about Passover, Rosh Hashanah, and Hanukkah. But do you know about Shavuot, Sukkot, or Yom Hashoah? You will find these and other Jewish holidays in *Dance, Sing, Remember: A Celebration of Jewish Holidays.*

Learning Extensions (Music and Dance)

Celebrations are happy times that are frequently observed with music and dance. Use directions on page 29 to teach children a popular dance called the hora. Use music such as authentic Israeli folk songs and dances, available from Amazon.com, as accompaniment.

16 ■ Holidays in General

Reudor, Jack Knight. *The Hebrew Months Tell Their Story.* New York: Pitspopany Press, 2000. 48p. $16.95. ISBN 1-930143-04-4.

 📖 PICTURE BOOK—Nonfiction; Jewish
Ages 7–12

Summary

Jewish history and holidays unfold in the stories of the Jewish months. Cartoonlike illustrations enliven an already lively text of poetry and prose highlighted with different colors of ink.

Booktalk

The Jewish calendar is a lunar calendar. Do you know what that means? A lunar calendar is based on the moon rather than the sun. What is the calendar we use in school? (Provide an opportunity for children to respond.) *The Hebrew Months Tell Their Story* presents the Jewish months and holidays (show the picture of the zodiac). Explain that each month features the sign of the zodiac for that month, a rhyme, facts about the month, and holidays that occur during that month.

Learning Extensions (Science)

Compare the Jewish lunar calendar with the Gregorian calendar based on the sun. Discuss why we use a calendar based on the sun rather than the moon. Have children research the history of the Gregorian calendar and when and why it was developed. Why is it called a Gregorian calendar rather than a solar calendar?

1.7 SPANISH

Fiestas in Mexico, Costa Rica, and the United States come to life with descriptions of celebrations such as Independence Day, Columbus Day, Oxcart Driver's Day, Holy Week, Virgin of the Angels, the Day of the Dead, and Three Kings' Day as well as Christmas and New Year's Day. Fireworks, parades, music, puppets, and foods are all part of the joyous activities. Dramatizations and art activities such as making clay figures, puppets, or painted oxcarts are among the suggested responses.

Ancona, George. *Fiesta Fireworks*. New York: Lothrop, Lee and Shepard Books, 1998. Unpaged. ISBN 0-688-14818-2.

    📖 PICTURE BOOK—Fiction; Mexico
Ages 7–12

Summary

Color photos help tell the story of how a little girl, her family, and neighborhood prepare for and celebrate a Mexican fiesta. An author's note tells of the town of Tultepec, its fireworks, and its patron saint.

Booktalk

The fiesta is about to begin! Grandfather is making fireworks. Caren and her mama are making a little bull for Caren to carry on her head. Uncle Leonardo and the men of the neighborhood are making a framework to hold the rockets. There will be a procession with bands playing, church bells ringing, and even puppets. Come! Join Caren and her family. The fiesta is about to begin.

Learning Extensions (Research Skills, Critical Thinking Skills, Language Arts)

Fireworks have been used through the centuries and around the world to celebrate special occasions. Discuss how fireworks are used in the United States in celebrations. Have children research the invention of fireworks in China and the development of pyrotechnics today. Introduce the book *The Fire-Maker's Daughter* by Philip Pullman, reviewed in *Bookwalks, Booktalks, and Read-Alouds*. Read *The Fire-Maker's Daughter,* then compare and contrast the early invention of fireworks in China with the development of pyrotechnics today and the fantasy and adventure tale of making fireworks in India.

Ancona, George. *Fiesta U.S.A.* New York: Lodestar Books, 1995. Unpaged. $15.99. ISBN 0-525-67498-5.

    📖 PICTURE BOOK—Nonfiction; Spanish
Ages 7–12

Summary

Four festivals celebrated in four communities—the Day of the Dead in San Francisco; Christmas in Albuquerque, New Mexico; New Year's Day in El Rancho, New Mexico; and Three Kings' Day in East Harlem, New York—focus on Latino culture in the United States.

Booktalk

You do not need to travel to Mexico or Puerto Rico to celebrate Spanish festivals. Celebrations can be found right here in the United States. The Day of the Dead, Christmas, New Year's Day, and Three Kings' Day are featured in *Fiesta U.S.A.* What is it that makes a fiesta a special celebration?

Learning Extensions (Language Arts)

Are there Spanish festivals being celebrated in your own community? Invite Spanish children in your group to describe their favorite festivals. Select a celebration such as Three Kings' Day and have the children research it. Make puppets, write a script, and act out the festival.

Roraff, Susan. *Festivals of the World: Costa Rica.* Milwaukee, Wis.: Gareth Stevens, 1999. 32p. $29.75. ISBN 0-8368-2022-3.

 PICTURE BOOK—Nonfiction; Costa Rica
 Ages 7–12

Summary

Color photographs supplement a calendar followed by brief descriptions of fiestas in Costa Rica. Directions for making pre-Columbian clay figures and a painted oxcart plus a recipe for fruit salad and a list of suggested readings complete the book.

Booktalk

This book celebrates fiesta on many occasions throughout the year, especially on Independence Day, Columbus Day, Oxcart Driver's Day, Holy Week (Good Friday and Judas Day), and Virgin of the

Angels. Some, such as Independence Day and Columbus Day, are weeklong celebrations. Others such as Oxcart Day, Holy Week and Virgin of the Angels are celebrated with parades, processions and even tricks.

Learning Extensions (Art)

Use the directions in the back of the book to make pre-Columbian clay figures or a painted oxcart. Prepare and serve fruit salad as a treat.

1.8 NORTH AMERICAN

Lena makes holiday hats for each month of the year, while Lenny and Mel share their antics as they celebrate Labor Day, Halloween, Thanksgiving, Christmas, New Year's Day, Valentine's Day, Presidents' Day, Cinco de Mayo, and Flag Day. Children can join them by making their own hats and writing stories about their own wacky holiday celebration.

Katz, Karen. *Twelve Hats for Lena: A Book of Months.* New York: Margaret K. McElderry Books, 2002. Unpaged. $16.95. ISBN 0-689-84873-0.

 PICTURE BOOK—Concept Book
 Ages 3–8

Summary

The author features her daughter Lena, who makes hats for each month of the year. Illustrations show Lena wearing a hat that tells more about the month, including the holidays that occur. Directions for making hats appear on the last page.

Read-Aloud

Read the story, focusing attention to the decorations on the hat that Lena is wearing. Introduce Lena and the materials she uses for making hats: paints, bows, flowers, and scissors. Read the text, introducing each month. Talk about the hats that Lena makes each month.

Learning Extensions (Art)

After reading the book, talk with the children about making a hat for a holiday that occurs in the current month, such as St. Patrick's Day in March. With the children, make a list of decorations to put on their hats and a list of materials to be used. Gather materials and have children make hats using the directions in the back of the book.

Kraft, Erik P. *Lenny and Mel: Holidazed!* New York: Simon & Schuster Books for Young Readers, 2002. 60p. $15.00. ISBN 0-689-84173-6.

    📖 CHAPTER BOOK—Fiction; United States
Ages 7–10

Summary

Lenny and Mel celebrate nine holidays: Labor Day, Halloween, Thanksgiving, Christmas, New Year's Day, Valentine's Day, Presidents' Day, Cinco de Mayo, and Flag Day. The boys' zany antics, humorous text, and cartoon illustrations are likely to appeal to reluctant readers.

Booktalk

What are those silly boys up to now? Mel's waving something on a broom. Lenny is right behind him banging a couple of pot lids together. Lenny and Mel have their own way of celebrating holidays. Sometimes they just don't get it! They make Valentine cards for their dog, use George Washington and Abraham Lincoln to celebrate Cinco de Mayo, and put Thanksgiving leftovers under their pillows for the Leftover Fairy. What will they think of next?

Learning Extensions (Language Arts)

Have children write imaginary stories about their own wacky holiday celebrations and share with the group.

2
January

INTRODUCTION

Civil rights leader Martin Luther King Jr. is honored on the third Monday in January. Titles chosen for this holiday tell the stories of King, as well as fictional civil rights workers. Suggested responses to the stories focus on dreams for a more peaceful community, dreams about what I can be, and discussions about integrity, decision making, and how children can make positive contributions to society. Selected titles and suggested responses can be incorporated into the curriculum through social studies, art, language arts, and character education.

Ramadan and Id-ul-Fitr are also included with January observances. Because the Muslim year is based on a lunar calendar, Ramadan, which is the fifth month, and Id-ul-Fitr, which is the first day of the sixth month, move backward through the Gregorian calendar. Ramadan is the Muslim holy month of fasting and ends with the feast of Id-ul-Fitr. The Muslim observance of Ramadan is a time of atonement, similar to the Jewish observance of Yom Kippur and the Christian observance of Lent. In contrast to Ramadan is Id-ul-Fitr, a celebration of gift giving, socializing, and feasting.

Titles chosen describe how a Muslim boy and an American Muslim family celebrate, briefly retell the story of the origin of the holidays, and include a historic novel that incorporates beliefs and practices of both Muslims and Hindus and the observance of Ramadan. Readers will have an opportunity to explore the practice of fasting, compare differing religious practices, and learn more about religious practices that are different from their own. Learning Extensions can be made through language arts and the development of research skills.

2.1 MARTIN LUTHER KING JR. DAY

The third Monday in January is a national holiday that honors the life and death of civil rights leader Martin Luther King Jr. His nonviolent leadership to extend equal rights to African-Americans culminated in the passage of the Civil Rights Act of 1964 and his assassination in 1968. Martin Luther King Jr. Day was first celebrated in 1986 after President Ronald Reagan signed a bill into law proclaiming the third Monday in January as a national holiday. School, federal offices, post offices, and banks close. Many communities celebrate by having parades and have honored King by naming streets for him.

Ansary, Mir Tamim. *Martin Luther King Jr. Day.* Des Plaines, Ill.: Heinemann Library, 1999. 32p. $19.92. ISBN 157572873-7.

 PICTURE BOOK—Nonfiction; African-American; Civil Rights
Ages 8–12

Summary

Each two-page spread features a photograph and text describing an aspect of the Martin Luther King Jr.'s life and efforts to promote the civil rights movement. The book begins by describing the holiday and introducing Martin Luther King Jr. and then gives a brief summary of slavery and the Civil War, segregation laws, and King's study of Mohandas Gandhi and concludes with the nonviolent events that led to the passage of the Civil Rights Act of 1964, culminating with King's death in 1968. Finally, a list of important dates begins with the slave trade that began in 1518 and ends with the nationwide celebration of Martin Luther King Jr. Day in 1986.

Booktalk

Do you have a hero? Martin Luther King Jr. was a hero and a great leader to many. Why? He fought to end injustice to African-Americans. He fought not with bullets or bombs but with words. Martin Luther King Jr. was a pacifist. Because of him, many unfair laws were changed. He was shot because he stood up for his beliefs.

His story is here. If you want to learn about a real hero, read *Martin Luther King Jr. Day.*

Learning Extensions (Social Studies, Art)

Martin Luther King Jr. dreamed of a world where all people shared equal rights and lived together in peace. Invite children to dream of a community (a library group, classroom, school, neighborhood, family, or town) where all members live together in peace. Group the children in pairs. Have them share their dreams with their partners and then draw posters to illustrate their dreams. Post the posters under the heading "Our Dreams for a More Peaceful Community" on the wall or in the hallway for all to see.

Farris, Christine King. *My Brother Martin: A Sister Remembers Growing Up with the Rev. Dr. Martin Luther King Jr.* New York: Simon & Schuster Books for Young Readers, 2003. Unpaged. Illustrated by Chris Soentpiet. $17.95. ISBN 0-689-84387-9.

  PICTURE BOOK—Nonfiction; Biography; African-American; Civil Rights
  All Ages

Summary

Martin Luther King Jr.'s sister writes about her brother as a little boy; their family, neighbors, and friends; the fun they had together; the mischief they got into; and the example of their father and mother. The book ends with a poem about Martin Luther King Jr., an afterword, and an illustrator's note.

Booktalk/Bookwalk

What would it be like to grow up with someone who is going to be famous? The author of this book is Martin Luther King Jr.'s sister. She shares her memories of growing up with her brother. Show and read aloud, "I have a dream ..." that appears on the frontispiece. Tell the children that when he was a boy, Martin Luther King Jr. promised his mother that "one day I'm going to turn this world upside down." Why would he make a promise like that? His sister tells the story of how he happened to make that promise and dream his dream for all children. Conclude by reading aloud the poem "You Can Be Like Martin: A Tribute to Dr. Martin Luther King Jr." in the back of the book.

Learning Extensions (Language Arts)

Follow up with a discussion based on the poem, that is, the lines "You can be an intelligent child....You can be a reader....You can be a speaker....You can pray in your own way....You can be a dreamer....You can be kind and loving...." Talk with the children about ways in which they can be intelligent; ways in which they can be readers, speakers, prayers, and dreamers; and ways in which they can be kind and loving. Then have each child write a poem about themselves using the lines "I can be ..."

Patrick, Denise Lewis. *A Lesson for Martin Luther King Jr.* New York: Aladdin Paperbacks, 2003. 32p. $4.00. ISBN 0-689-85397-1.

 CHAPTER BOOK—Nonfiction; Biography; African-American; Civil Rights
Ages 5–7

Summary

When Martin Luther King Jr.'s friend Bobby said that he could no longer play with Martin because Martin was black and Bobby was white, Martin decided to change the rules.

Booktalk

It's the first day of school, and Martin wants to show his book to his friend Bobby. Bobby said, "Maybe later." When Martin took Bobby some fresh, homemade chocolate chip cookies, Bobby said, "I can't." Is Bobby mad at Martin? Martin decides to ask.

Learning Extensions (Social Studies, Character Education)

Ask children if there is someone they treat differently from others because of skin color, religion, disability, the clothes they wear, where they live, or for some other reason. How can they change the rules and change their behavior? Consider using this book as part of your character education program.

Robinet, Harriette Gillem. *Walking to the Bus-Rider Blues.* New York: Aladdin Paperbacks, 2002. 146p. $4.99. ISBN 0-689-83886-7.

 📖 CHAPTER BOOK—Fiction; African-American; Civil Rights
 📖 *Ages 8–12*

Summary

This is a story based on events in Martin Luther King Jr.'s life. The mystery of the disappearing rent money, coupled with the story of African-American life in Montgomery, Alabama, during the bus boycott of 1956, makes for spellbinding, fast-paced reading.

Booktalk

It's 1956 in Montgomery, Alabama. Martin Luther King Jr. is the new minister at Dexter Avenue Baptist Church. For six months, the African-American community has been making a nonviolent protest against segregation, walking rather than riding the city buses. Alfa, Alfa's sister Zinnia, and their great grandmother Big Mama have money problems. Their rent money is disappearing. It looks as if someone is stealing it. Can Reverend King's philosophy of nonviolence help them solve the mystery?

Learning Extensions (Character Education)

Engage students in a discussion of the meaning of phrases such as "nonviolent protest," "walk the walk and talk the talk of nonviolence," and "talking the talk of love." Ask students if they have had any experiences in their lives that are examples of these phrases or if they know of other examples from history. Consider using this book as part of your character education program in conjunction with the character trait of integrity. Ask students to think of situations in their own lives in which they can put these phrases into practice.

Other Books to Use for Martin Luther King Jr. Day

McWhorter, Diane. *A Dream of Freedom: The Civil Rights Movement from 1954 to 1918.* New York: Scholastic, 2004. Ages 10 and up. 160p. $19.95. ISBN 0-439-57678-4.

Peck, Ira. *The Life and Words of Martin Luther King, Jr.* New York: Scholastic, 2000. Ages 8–12. 112p. $4.50. ISBN 0-590-43827-1.

Reid, Robin. *Thank You, Dr. King!* New York: Simon Spotlight/Nick Jr., 2003. Ages 4–8. Unpaged. Illustrated by Dan Kanemoto. $3.50. ISBN 0-689-85242-8.

2.2 RAMADAN AND ID-UL-FITR

Because the Muslim year is based on a lunar calendar, Ramadan and Id-ul-Fitr rotate backward through the Gregorian calendar. The dates on which they occur change yearly. Ramadan, the fifth month of the Muslim year, is a holy month of fasting. Muslims believe that it was during Ramadan that the angel Gabriel dictated the Qu'ran to Muhammad. Like the Christian observance of Lent and the Jewish observance of Yom Kippur, the Muslim observance of Ramadan is a time of atonement. Id-ul-Fitr means "breaking of the fast" and marks the end of Ramadan and the beginning of a new month. It is celebrated with prayers, feasting, wearing of new or clean clothes, socializing, and the giving of alms and gifts.

Ghazi, Suhaib Hamid. *Ramadan.* New York: Holiday House, 1996. Unpaged. Illustrated by Omar Rayyan. $15.95. ISBN 0-8234-1254-7.

 PICTURE BOOK—Nonfiction; Muslim
Ages 7–12

Summary

Arabic characters and Islamic patterns border the illustrations and text that explain how Hakeem, a young Muslim boy, and his family observe the month of Ramadan by fasting from food and drink during daylight hours.

Booktalk

Hakeem is a Muslim boy. During the month of Ramadan, he and his family, with all their Muslim friends, fast—they do not eat food or drink from sunup to sundown. They eat a big breakfast before daylight and a large meal after dark. After the evening meal, many pray together at the mosque. Ramadan is a holy month of fasting. Do people other than Muslims observe a time of prayer and fasting? How does Ramadan compare with other observances?

Learning Extensions (Research Skills, Language Arts)

Have children explore, in the library or on the Internet, the practice of fasting. When did this practice arise? Why do people fast? What people other than Muslims fast? What are the health consequences of fasting? Have children orally share their findings with the entire group.

Hoyt-Goldsmith, Diane. *Celebrating Ramadan.* New York: Holiday House, 2001. 32p. Photographs by Lawrence Migdale. $17.95. ISBN 0-8234-1581-3.

  PICTURE BOOK—Nonfiction; Muslim
  Ages 7–12

Summary

This book features an American Muslim family and their celebration of Ramadan and Id-ul-Fitr. Beginning with a brief description of the religion of Islam and a map showing the countries in which Islam is practiced, followed by a brief explanation of Muhammad's Revelations and the Qu'ran, this book continues with a description of Islamic daily prayer, the Ramadan fast, and finally the celebration of Id-ul-Fitr that marks the end of Ramadan. A cookie recipe is included in the text, and the book concludes with a glossary.

Booktalk

Come! Meet Ibraheem. He is in the fourth grade and lives near Princeton, New Jersey. He and his family are Muslims who fast during the month of Ramadan. During Ramadan, Muslims do not eat or drink during daylight hours. When Ramadan ends, they celebrate Id-ul-Fitr with prayers, gifts, and special foods. Just what are Ramadan and Id-ul-Fitr? To find out, read *Celebrating Ramadan.*

Learning Extensions (Language Arts, Social Studies)

Engage children in a discussion of their family religious practices. Do they observe times of fasting, prayer, and gift giving? Compare Islamic practices of fasting, prayer, and gift giving with Jewish, Christian, and other religious traditions. Encourage children to gather information by talking with friends and neighbors and by researching books and the Internet. Use the recipe in the book to bake and serve the cookie, which is named Ghorayyibah.

Kerven, Rosalind. *Id-ul-Fitr.* Austin, Tex.: Raintree Steck-Vaughn, 1997. 30p. $27.79. ISBN 0-8172-4609-6.

 PICTURE BOOK—Nonfiction; Muslim
 Ages 7–12

Summary

Color photos accompany and describe Ramadan, the story of Muhammad, the angel Jibril (Gabriel), and the origins of the Qu'ran and explain the celebration of Id-ul-Fitr. The book ends with a recipe for Id pudding, directions for making an Id card, a glossary, and suggestions for further reading.

Booktalk

Have you ever gone without food—on purpose? How might you feel if you were not allowed to eat or drink during daylight hours for a whole month? Older children and adults who practice the religion of Islam fast during the month of Ramadan. When Ramadan ends, they celebrate the feast of Id-ul-Fitr. What kind of celebration do you suppose that is? Let's find out in *Id-ul-Fitr.*

Learning Extensions (Research Skills, Language Arts)

Encourage children to learn more about Ramadan, Muhammad, and the Qu'ran by forming three small groups. Have each small group research the topic assigned to them and report back to the whole group. Use the recipe on page 28 to make and serve Id pudding.

Lasky, Kathryn. *Jahanara: Princess of Princesses, India 1627.* New York: Scholastic, 2002. 192p. $10.95. ISBN 0-439-22350-4.

📖 CHAPTER BOOK—Fiction; Muslim and Hindu
Ages 9–14

Summary

Jahanara records in her diary her innermost thoughts and feelings, hopes, and dreams about her life in the royal palaces of the Moghul court and on military campaigns; the treachery of her brother, Aurangzeb, and her grandmother, Nur Mahal; and the love of her father, Shah Jahan, for his wife, Mumtaz Mahal, that moved him to build the Taj Mahal. Beliefs and practices of Muslims and Hindus, including the observance of Ramadan, provide a backdrop for the diary entries that begins with the family's imprisonment and release in 1627 when Jahanara is 13 years old and end with her mother's death in 1631 when Jahanara is 17 years old.

Booktalk

It is only the eighth day of Ramadan, yet Jahanara is so hungry that she can think of nothing but food. She and her brother, Dara, make a list of their favorite foods. Both are too distracted by their thoughts of food to pay attention to their studies. Dara devises a plan to sneak food from the kitchen. With the help of a eunuch, a cook slips sweetmeats to Jahanara. Jahanara is worried. She fears that her brother Aurangzeb knows about the secret food. What will happen to the cook? Will he be punished?

Learning Extensions (Critical Thinking, Research Skills)

To encourage understanding and appreciation for Central Asia and for Muslim and Hindu beliefs and practices, have children create two charts: one of Muslim beliefs and practices, the other of Hindu beliefs and practices. Revisit the text to find information. Since this story is set in the past, it might be helpful to have children research current practices and some of the diversity within Islam and Hinduism.

Focus on Central Asia by using the historical note, the Moghul dynasty family tree, and illustrations to make connections between the seeds of unrest sown by Aurangzeb between Muslims and Hindus, the creation of the separate countries of Pakistan and India following independence from British rule in 1947, and Pakistan's ties with Afghanistan. For more information about Hindu beliefs and practices, see the books reviewed in chapter 1.

Other Books to Use for Ramadan

Demi. *Muhammad.* New York: Margaret K. McElderry Books, 2003. Ages 4–8. 39p. ISBN 0-689-852649.

Douglass, Susan. *Ramadan.* Minneapolis: Carolrhoda Books, 2003. Ages 4–8. 48p. Illustrated by Jeni Reeves. $5.95. ISBN 1-575-055848.

Matthews, Mary. *Magid Fasts for Ramadan.* New York: Clarion Books, 2000. 48p. Illustrated by E. B. Lewis. $6.95. ISBN 0-618-040358.

3
February

INTRODUCTION

February is National African-American History Month. This is a time to honor the achievements of African-Americans and to recognize their role in the political, social, and economic development of the United States. Of the four new books about African-Americans selected for inclusion, one chronicles the history of the black soldier beginning with Africans who accompanied Christopher Columbus and ending with those who fought in Kuwait. Another tells the story of Fisk University's Jubilee Singers, who tour the country raising money for their school. A third tells the story of a freed slave family who founded a town called Freedom. The fourth tells the history of slavery from its earliest beginnings in Sumeria 5,000 years ago to examples of its existence in parts of the world today.

Four holidays also occur in February when winter is getting long. The groundhog forecasts the weather. If it sees its shadow on Groundhog Day, winter will continue for another six weeks! But winter or not, there are celebrations to look forward to (the Chinese New Year and Valentine's Day) and presidents to honor on Presidents' Day. Fiction and nonfiction titles explore origins and practices related to Groundhog Day, Chinese New Year, Valentine's Day, and Presidents' Day. Learning activities include developing an outdoor garden plot or planting seeds in pots on the patio or windowsill, making Valentines, developing a list of rules to live, and other activities across the curriculum.

3.1 NATIONAL AFRICAN-AMERICAN HISTORY MONTH

National African-American History Month originated in 1926 as Negro History Week. Dr. Carter G. Woodson, an African-American author and scholar, chose February, the month we celebrate the birthdays of Frederick Douglas and Abraham Lincoln, to focus on the achievements of African-Americans. When the United States celebrated its bicentennial in 1976, the observance of Negro History Week was extended from one week to the entire month and the name changed to Black History Month. Gradually, the name National African-American History Month came into common usage. Each year, the president of the United States issues a proclamation and names the theme for the year that has been established by the Association for the Study of Afro-American Life and History. Around the country, programs and activities honor the achievements and contributions of African-Americans.

Clinton, Catherine. *The Black Soldier: 1492 to the Present.* Boston: Houghton Mifflin, 2000. 117p. $17.00. ISBN 0-395-67722-X.

 CHAPTER BOOK—Nonfiction; African-American
 Ages 10–14

Summary

Fifteen chapters of text and photographs chronicle the history of the black soldier beginning with the Africans who accompanied Christopher Columbus on his voyages to the New World and Vasco Nunez de Balboa, Hernando Cortes, Francisco Pizarro, and other Spanish explorers who came after Columbus. Black soldiers continued to play a role during the colonial period, the Revolutionary and Civil Wars, and the opening of the western frontier and again during the Spanish-American War, World Wars I and II, and the Korean, Vietnam, and Gulf Wars.

Booktalk

In 1994, General Colin Powell addressed the graduating class at Howard University, identifying himself "as a direct descendant of the Buffalo Soldiers and of the Tuskegee Airmen." Who were the Buffalo Soldiers and the Tuskegee Airmen? You have heard about Christopher Columbus. Have you heard about his African-born navigator, Pedro Alonso Nino, and his African crew member, Diego Mendez? What about the Africans who accompanied Vasco Nunez de Balboa, Hernando Cortes, and Francisco Pizarro as they explored the New World? In this book, you'll learn about the courage and contributions of black soldiers in America—from the colonial period and the Revolutionary War through the Civil War, World Wars I and II, and the Korean, Vietnam, and Gulf Wars.

Learning Extensions (Language Arts, Social Studies)

Have children interview family members, friends, and neighbors about their military experiences as or with African-American soldiers. Prepare a program with children retelling those experiences. Extend the book by showing and discussing the video *The Tuskegee Airmen*.

Hopkinson, Deborah. *A Band of Angels.* New York: Aladdin Paperbacks, 2002. Unpaged. Illustrated by Raul Colon. $6.99. ISBN 0-689-84887.

 PICTURE BOOK—Historical Fiction
 Ages 5–9

Summary

The Jubilee Singers at Fisk University was formed in 1871 when a group of Fisk students set out on a singing tour to raise money for the school. This fictional account of the beginning of the Jubilee Singers is told from the perspective of the young great-great-granddaughter of one of the singers.

Booktalk

The Jubilee Singers from Fisk University have been singing songs for more than 100 years—beautiful songs, like "Swing Low, Sweet Chariot" and "Go Down, Moses." Great-great-Grandma Ella Sheppard was one of the first Jubilee Singers. In 1871, she and her friends toured the country, singing to raise money for their school, Fisk College. The school needed $5,000 to keep their doors open. The roof leaked, and the rooms were cold and damp. On what they thought was the last night of their tour, the singers had raised only $500. In desperation, Ella Sheppard bravely went out on stage. Would she be able to save the day?

Learning Extensions (Music)

Some of the spirituals sung by the Jubilee Singers are listed in the back of the book. Play recordings by the Jubilee Singers. (The audio CD *In Bright Memories* is available from Amazon.com. Another source is Overstock.com.) Learn to sing some of their songs. For more information about the Jubilee Singers, see www.pbs.org and the Fisk University Web site at www.fisk.edu.

Sanders, Scott Russell. *A Place Called Freedom.* New York: Aladdin Paperbacks, 2001. Unpaged. Illustrated by Thomas B. Allen. $5.99. ISBN 0-689-84001-2.

 PICTURE BOOK—Historic Fiction
 Ages 5–8

Summary

Gentle illustrations and lyrical language tell the story of the freed slave family who made their way from Tennessee to Indiana to make a new life and found a town called Freedom.

Booktalk

Yes, there really is a place called Freedom. My dad founded the town. My aunts, uncles, and cousins and a lot of other folks came to live there. We built a church, a store, a stable, and a mill. Our village grew until the railroad ran tracks through our town. Now we needed a name. Folks wanted to name our town Starman after my dad, but he said no. Why do you suppose he wanted to name it Freedom?

Learning Extensions (Social Studies, Map Skills, Research Skills)

Have your children find the town of Freedom, Indiana, on a map. (It is west of Bloomington, in Owen County on the Wabash River.) If there is a town named Freedom in your state, have your children find it on the map. (California, Nebraska, New Hampshire, Oklahoma,

Pennsylvania, and Wisconsin all have towns named Freedom.) Have children research how the town in your state got its name. If you do not have a town named Freedom in your state, have children research the origins of the name of the town you live in.

Watkins, Richard. *Slavery: Bondage Throughout History.* Boston: Houghton Mifflin, 2001. 136p. $18.00. ISBN 0-395-02289-5.

 CHAPTER BOOK—Nonfiction
 Ages 10–14.

Summary

Fifteen chapters chronicle the history of human bondage from the beginnings of civilization in Sumeria 5,000 years ago to the chattel slavery identified by Anti-Slavery International in Sudan and Mauritania; forced child labor in the production of carpets in Pakistan, India, and Nepal; and forced child prostitution in Southeast Asia.

Booktalk

The Emancipation Proclamation freed the slaves in the United States. But when did slavery begin? *Slavery: Bondage Throughout History* describes the presence of slavery, which started a long time ago—in some of the earliest civilizations. It spread into the Greek and Roman empires across Europe and throughout Africa and the Muslim world. Why did something as terrible as slavery ever start? How did it come to an end? And has slavery really been eliminated from today's world?

Learning Extensions (Social Studies, Research Skills)

The history of slavery is also the history of human thinking. Engage children in discussing the development of the thinking that first supported then opposed slavery as a social, economic, and political institution. What is today's thinking regarding rights for all people? What other rights do we have in this country? Have children research the Bill of Rights and the UN Declaration of Human Rights and compare the two documents.

Other Books to Use for National African-American History Month

Bryan, Ashley. *All Night, All Day: A Child's First Book of African-American Spirituals.* New York: Aladdin Paperbacks, 1991, 2004. Ages 4–8. Unpaged. Musical arrangements by David Manning Thomas. $6.99. ISBN 0-689-86786-7.

McGill Alice. *Molly Bannaky.* Boston: Houghton Mifflin, 1999. Ages 4–8. Unpaged. Illustrated by Chris K. Soentpiet. $16.00. ISBN 0-395-72287-0.

McKissack, Patricia, and Frederick McKissack. *Black Hand, White Sails: The Story of African-American Whalers.* New York: Scholastic, 1999. Ages 10 and up. 147p. $15.95. ISBN 0-590-48313-7.

3.2 GROUNDHOG DAY

Groundhog Day is observed on February 2. Tradition has it that if the groundhog sees its shadow there will be six more weeks of winter. The observance of Groundhog Day has its origins in Indian lore mixed with the Christian observance of Candlemas Day. The Delaware Indians who settled near Punxsutawney, Pennsylvania, in 1723 considered Wojak, the groundhog, to be their ancestral grandfather. German settlers who came in the early 1700s brought their Christian observance of Candlemas Day. Candlemas Day falls halfway between winter and spring on February 2. Clergy blessed candles and gave them to the people who placed a lighted candle in the window. If the sun came out on Candlemas Day, there would be six more weeks of wintry weather. The first reference to Groundhog Day appeared in 1841 in the diary of James Morris, a storekeeper in Morgantown, Pennsylvania. On February 2, 1886, a proclamation in the Punxsutawney newspaper marked the first official celebration of Groundhog Day.

Birenbaum, Barbara. *Groundhog Willie's Shadow.* Clearwater, Fla.: Peartree, 2001. 29p. $19.95. ISBN 0935343-74-1.

  PICTURE BOOK—Nonfiction
  Ages 8–12

Summary

Two stories appear side by side in parallel columns about Willie of Wiarton, Ontario, the official groundhog of Canada. The stories begin with the Mohawk legend about Klionda, the Indian, and Nawgeentuck, the groundhog and the origin of Groundhog Day in Canada. The stories continue with accounts of groundhog sightings and shadow castings by Willie; Punxsutawney Phil; Jimmy of Sun Prairie, Wisconsin; Essex Ed from West Orange, New Jersey; Harley from Greensboro, North Carolina; and Octoraro Orphie from Quarryville, Pennsylvania. The book ends with e-mail addresses for Willie and Phil, suggestions for further reading, and a dictionary.

Booktalk

Punxsutawney Phil is the groundhog from Punxsutawney, Pennsylvania, who makes the news each year on Groundhog Day. But Punxsutawney Phil is not the only groundhog that predicts weather. Willie of Wiarton, Ontario; Essex Ed of West Orange, New Jersey; and many other groundhogs forecast the weather. Do you know the story of how Groundhog Day started? It's all here in *Groundhog Willie's Shadow.*

Learning Extensions (Language Arts, Research Skills)

Visit the Web sites given for Willie and Phil in the back of the book (www.wiarton-willie.org and pcoc@penn.com) for more information about groundhogs and Groundhog Day. Some children might want to e-mail Willie or Phil at willie@bmts.com or pcoc@penn.com. Have children prepare oral reports using the information they have gathered.

Cherry, Lynne. *How Groundhog's Garden Grew.* New York: Blue Sky Press, 2003. Unpaged. $15.95. ISBN 0-439-32371-1.

 PICTURE BOOK—Fiction
 Ages 5–10

Summary

Groundhog stole food from his friends' gardens until Squirrel offered to teach him how to make his own garden. With that, the life cycle of the garden ecosystem unfolds: plants, insects, birds, and animals. Front- and endpapers show rows of vegetables growing. Some pages in the text are bordered with illustrations of vegetables, plants, and insects. Of particular note are the illustrations that authentically represent the garden, plants, animals, and birds.

Bookwalk

Groundhog has no garden, so he eats vegetables from his neighbor's garden until Squirrel scolds him. Then Groundhog's life changes! Show children the book, turn the pages, and talk about the illustrations showing Squirrel teaching Groundhog how to garden. Call attention to Groundhog's garden with tall plants in back and short plants in front. Finally, show the endpapers and encourage children to name the vegetables that are illustrated.

Learning Extensions (Science)

Celebrate Groundhog Day by having children plant an assortment of seeds, such as beans, peas, and lettuce. Have them record the time it takes for the different seeds to sprout. Some children may want to draw pictures of the young sprouts using the illustrations as guide. If you are gardening in pots on the windowsills, sprout seeds in clear plastic cups using cotton to hold the seeds in place against the clear plastic. Keep the cotton moist. Watch the seeds send out roots as well as sprout. Compare and contrast the rooting and sprouting of the beans, peas, and lettuce seeds.

Resources for Gardening

For more information about gardening, write to the Center for Environmental Education. The address is in the back of the book. Or visit www.cee-ane.org, www.kidsgrowingfood.org., or www.nga.org. Additional resources from Libraries Unlimited, Inc., are *Beyond the Bean Seed: Gardening Activities for Grades K–6* and *Cultivating a Child's Imagination Through Gardening.*

Other Books to Use for Groundhog Day

Bassett, Jeni. *It's Groundhog Day!* New York: Scholastic, 1991. Ages 4–8. 32p. $3.50. ISBN 0-590-44669-X.

McMullan, Kate. *Fluffy Meets the Groundhog.* New York: Scholastic, 2002. Ages 4–8. 40p. $3.99. ISBN 0-439-20672-3.

3.3 CHINESE NEW YEAR

Chinese New Year, popularly known as the Spring Festival, is based on the lunar calendar, so it does not occur on the same date every year. It is celebrated for 15 days. Preparations begin a month in advance with cleaning, decorating, buying gifts, and preparing food. New Year's Eve is celebrated with a feast of seafood, dumplings, and special foods and an evening of games followed by midnight fireworks. On New Year's Day, married couples give children and unmarried adults money in red envelopes. After 15 days, the celebration ends with the Festival of Lanterns.

Waters, Kate, and Madeline Slovenz-Low. *Lion Dancer: Ernie Wan's Chinese New Year.* New York: Scholastic, 1990. Unpaged. Photographs by Martha Cooper. $13.00. ISBN 0-590-43047-5.

 PICTURE BOOK—Nonfiction
  Ages 7–12

Summary

Color photographs and text describe how Ernie Wan and his family prepare for Chinese New Year. Ernie performs his first Lion Dance in his father's kung fu school and then in the streets of New York City.

Bookwalk

Introduce Ernie to your children by pointing to his picture on the cover. Turn the pages, show the pictures, and tell the children that Ernie lives in New York City. He attends public school, Chinese school, and kung fu school. This year, Ernie is celebrating Chinese New Year by performing the Lion Dance for the first time. Ernie works hard to always keep the lion moving. He must keep his own mouth and ears covered because of the noise and the smoke from the firecrackers. Look how spectacular the dance is.

Learning Extensions (Language Arts)

Use the Chinese horoscope in the back of the book to find the year each child was born and name the animal of that year. What are the characteristics of people born in that year? Ask the children how they fit those characteristics.

Wong, Janet S. *This Next New Year.* New York: Frances Foster Books, 2000. Unpaged. Illustrated by Yangsook Choi. $16.00. ISBN 0-374-35503-7.

 📖 PICTURE BOOK—Fiction; Asian American
  Ages 4–8

Summary

A little boy prepares to celebrate Chinese New Year. The customs of cooking special foods, cleaning the house, wearing new clothes, and lighting firecrackers are all part of the ritual of clearing away the bad luck, making room for the good luck, and preparing for a new beginning. An author's note at the end tells more about Chinese New Year symbols and customs.

Booktalk

When is New Year's Day? If you said January 1, you're only partly right. Chinese New Year occurs anywhere from January 21 to February 19. Glenn and Evelyn celebrate every year. Glenn is French and German. His family celebrates by eating take-out Thai food. Evelyn is Hopi and Mexican. She likes to get red envelopes stuffed with money. I'm Chinese and Korean. My family celebrates Chinese New Year in a big, big way! We even have firecrackers. What else do you think we do? Read *This Next New Year* and see for yourself.

Learning Extensions (Language Arts, Critical Thinking Skills)

Read aloud, show the pictures, and plan a Chinese New Year celebration. You may want to compare and contrast the Chinese New Year custom of cleaning away the bad luck with the Jewish New Year (Rosh Hashanah) custom of casting off sin through repentance and forgiveness. Use a Venn diagram to make the comparison. Have children research when New Year's Day is celebrated for different groups of people, such as Jews, Muslims, and so on.

Other Books to Use for Chinese New Year

Demi. *Happy, Happy Chinese New Year!* New York: Crown Books for Young Readers, 2003. Ages 4–8. 24p. $8.95. ISBN 0-375-826424.

Hoyt-Goldsmith, Diane. *Celebrating Chinese New Year.* New York: Holiday House, 1999. Ages 4–8. 32p. $6.95. ISBN 0-823-415201.

3.4 VALENTINE'S DAY

Beginning in the fifth century, February 14 was celebrated in honor of a Catholic bishop named Valentine. Before he was led to his death, Valentine signed a message to his jailer's daughter, "From Your Valentine." Roman men developed the tradition of using Valentine's name to send messages of affection to the women they admired. In 1415, when Charles, Duke of Orleans, was imprisoned in the Tower of London, he sent his wife the first official Valentine card. The practice of sending cards to friends and loved ones has continued to this day.

Carr, Jan. *Sweet Hearts.* New York: Holiday House, 2003. Unpaged. Illustrated by Dorothy Donohue. $16.00. ISBN 0-8234-1732-8.

 PICTURE BOOK—Fiction
 Ages 3–7

Summary

Little Bear makes and decorates heart Valentines for Mommy, Daddy, Grandma, baby, and the dog. An introduction gives a brief history of Valentine's Day. Instructions are given in the back of the book for making and decorating heart Valentines.

Read-Aloud

The short, rhythmic text on each page lends itself to reading aloud. Read aloud and show the pictures.

Learning Extensions (Art)

Use the instructions in the back of the book to have the children make and decorate heart Valentines like Little Bear.

Landau, Elaine. *Valentine's Day: Candy, Love, and Hearts.* Berkeley Heights, N.J.: Enslow Publishers, 2002. 48p. $23.93. ISBN 0-7660-1779-6.

 📖 CHAPTER BOOK—Nonfiction
 Ages 8–12

Summary

Five chapters explain the origins of Valentine's Day and the popularity of sending cards and then describe special weddings and celebrations around the world. Instructions for making Heart People Cards, a glossary, suggested readings, and Internet addresses complete the book.

Booktalk

What do we do on Valentine's Day? We send cards and give flowers or candy to the people we like and love. Valentine's Day is also a popular day for weddings—all kinds of weddings, be they in hot-air balloons, on roller coasters, or even underwater. In some communities, such as Loveland, Colorado, and Valentine, Nebraska, the whole town celebrates. How did Valentine's Day get started, and why do we celebrate the way we do?

Learning Extensions (Art)

Have children use the instructions in the back of the book to make Heart People Cards. Serve heart-shaped candies for a treat. For more crafts, games, and cards, go to www.kidsdomain.com/holiday/val/index.html, which is listed in the back of the book. To send e-cards from Valentine, Nebraska, have children go to www.heartcity.net/ecards, which is also listed in the back of the book.

Ross, Kathy. *All New Crafts for Valentine's Day.* Brookfield, Conn.: Millbrook Press, 2002. 48p. Illustrated by Barbara Leonard. ISBN $16.00. 0-7613-2553-0.

 📖 PICTURE BOOK—Nonfiction
 Ages 5–10

Summary

Clear, specific, colorful directions for 20 simple Valentine crafts, such as Valentines and a holder, a bookmark, a wind chime, a crown, and others, invite children to cut, paste, paint, and color a variety of creative projects.

Bookwalk

Generate interest in the book by showing the pictures and telling the children that this book has directions for making Valentine crafts, such as a butterflies garland (pages 8–9), a Hearts Dog Valentine (pages 13–15), and a Changing Message Magnet (pages 26–27).

Learning Extensions (Art)

Use the directions in the book to create a Valentine project, such as a Party Blower Valentine. Both boys and girls are likely to enjoy the fun of creating hidden messages using stickers and markers.

Thompson, Lauren. *Mouse's First Valentine.* New York: Simon & Schuster Books for Young Readers, 2002. Unpaged. Illustrated by Buket Erdogan. $12.95. ISBN 0-689-84724-6.

 PICTURE BOOK—Fiction
 Ages 2–6

Summary

Little Mouse watches big sister Minka gather materials and make a Valentine.

Read-Aloud

The simple text with the repetitive line "What could it be? wondered Mouse." lends itself to reading aloud. Read aloud and show the pictures. Pause at each "What could it be? wondered Mouse." and encourage children to guess what it could be.

Learning Extensions (Art)

Gather enough red paper, white lace, ribbon, and paste for each child in your group. After reading aloud, show the children how to make Valentines just like Minka did.

Other Books to Use for Valentine's Day

Gantos, Jack. *Rotten Ralph's Rotten Romance.* Boston: Houghton Mifflin, 2004. Ages 4–8. 32p. Illustrated by Nicole Rubel. $5.95. ISBN 0-618-49486-3.

Tompert, Ann. *Saint Valentine.* Honesdale, Pa.: Boyds Mills Press, 2004. Ages 6 and up. 32p. Illustrated by Kestutis Kasparavicius. $15.95. ISBN 1-59078-181-3.

Wilson, Karma, and Suzanne Watts. *Bear Hugs: Romantically Ridiculous Animal Rhymes.* New York: Margaret K. McElderry Books, 2005. Ages 4–8. Unpaged. $14.95. ISBN 0-689-85763-2.

3.5 PRESIDENTS' DAY

Since 1971, Presidents' Day, officially known as Washington's Birthday, has been observed on the third Monday of February in honor of George Washington, Abraham Lincoln, and all other presidents. Washington's Birthday was first observed February 22, 1796, to celebrate George Washington's birthday. It became a national holiday by the early 1800s. In 1865, Abraham Lincoln's birthday was celebrated on February 12. Although Lincoln's birthday did not become a national holiday like Washington's, it did become a legal holiday in several states. In 1968, legislation shifted the observance of Washington's Birthday to the third Monday of February. Popular usage and practice refer to this day as Presidents' Day, a time to honor all presidents.

Schmidt, Suzy. *Abraham Lincoln.* New York: Scholastic, 2002. Unpaged. Illustrated by David A. Johnson. $16.95. ISBN 0-590-93566-6.

 📖 PICTURE BOOK—Nonfiction
  Ages 6–12

Summary

Rhythmic text, peppered with quotations and colloquial expressions and stylized watercolor illustrations, retells the story of Abraham Lincoln's life from birth to death. A time line of important dates in his life appears at the end of the book.

Booktalk

Introduce the book by showing the children a penny and asking them if they know who the man on the penny is. Encourage them to talk about what they know about the man. Then begin your Booktalk by saying, "That's right. The man on the penny wasn't always on the penny. He is Abraham Lincoln. He was born in Kentucky, then moved with his family to Indiana. He went to school 'by littles' for no more than a year in all. He grew up working the fields and reading whatever he could, whenever, wherever he could. As a young man he worked at whatever jobs were available and studied surveying and law. He went on to become the sixteenth president of the United States. Do you know what he was referring to when he said, 'If my name ever goes into history, it will be for this act'?"

Learning Extensions (Social Studies, Language Arts, Research Skills)

Use the time line at the end of the book as a guide to retelling the story of Abraham Lincoln. Select 17 students. Have each student choose or assign to each student one of the important dates in the time line. Have students re-read and retell the events associated with each date. Older students can be encouraged to conduct further research on their events and write a report about their findings.

Harness, Cheryl. *Ghosts of the White House.* New York: Aladdin Paperbacks, 2001. Unpaged. $6.99. ISBN 0-689-84892-7.

 PICTURE BOOK—Nonfiction
 Ages 7–10

Summary

Text, illustrations, dialogue bubbles, sidebars, and a time line provide lively information about the presidents of the United States, important events that occurred during their time in office, and the White House.

Booktalk

Come with Sara! George Washington will introduce you to 35 presidents of the United States. Let's take a tour of the White House and learn more about our country's history and its leaders.

Learning Extensions (Social Studies, Language Arts)

This book lends itself to a number of responses. Some students might want to reconstruct the time line in the book to post on the library, media center, or classroom wall. Others might want to construct a board game based on information in the book. Still others might want to create a game by enlarging the profiles of the presidents in the back of the book.

Van Steenwyk, Elizabeth. *When Abraham Talked to the Trees.* Grand Rapids, Mich.: Eerdmans Books for Young Readers. 2000. Unpaged. Illustrated by Bill Farnsworth. $16.00. ISBN 0-8028-5191-6.

    PICTURE BOOK—Nonfiction
    Ages 6–12

Summary

Soft oil paintings illustrate the anecdotal text that tells of Abraham Lincoln's love of words beginning with the book left to him by his mother and continuing with the books of his stepmother; the preaching he heard on Sundays; his efforts to write in the ashes, dirt, and snow; and finally his own public speaking that came to fruition in his public life.

Booktalk

Abe loved words. His mother left him one book. He read it again and again and again. At the end of the day when the other children were asleep, Abe read by the light of the fire the books that belonged to his stepmother. He recited to his family the book by Aesop and read Webster's dictionary and the Bible. He told stories to the other children; practiced writing in the ashes, dirt, and snow; and practiced the preacher's sermons alone in the woods. Abraham Lincoln tucked the words away inside of him. He knew he might need them one day when people would listen to what he had to say.

Learning Extensions (Social Studies, Language Arts)

What did Abraham Lincoln have to say? What did people listen to? Use this book as a lead to a unit on the Gettysburg Address or the Emancipation Proclamation. Develop public speaking skills by having students orally practice and deliver the Gettysburg Address. Younger students could memorize and recite a different portion of the speech.

Washington, George. *George-isms.* New York: Atheneum Books for Young Readers. 2000. 80p. $7.95. ISBN 0-689-84082-9.

 📖 QUOTATIONS—Nonfiction
  All Ages

Summary

The 110 rules of civility and decent behavior that George Washington wrote out when he was 14 years old are set forth in this little book. Many will seem quaint, humorous, or outdated. Others still provide guidance for life today.

Booktalk

When George Washington was 14 years old, he wrote out a set of rules to live by. That was a long time ago. What rules would you write?

Learning Extensions (Social Studies, Language Arts)

Ask children why they think George Washington chose to live by a list of rules. Then ask the children if they are expected to observe certain rules at home or in school. Next have children work in pairs to develop a list of five rules that they would like to live by. Finally, have children share their lists of rules with the entire group.

Other Books to Use for Presidents' Day

Borden, Louise. *A. Lincoln and Me.* New York: Scholastic, 1999. Ages 7–10. Unpaged. Illustrated by Ted Lewin. $15.95. ISBN 0-590-45714-4.

Cheney, Lynne. *When Washington Crossed the Delaware: A Wintertime Story for Young Patriots.* New York: Simon & Schuster Books for Young Readers, 2004. All ages. Unpaged. Illustrated by Peter M. Fiore. $16.95. ISBN 0-689-87043-4.

O'Connor, Jane. *If the Walls Could Talk: Family Life at the White House.* Simon & Schuster Books for Young Readers, 2004. Ages 6–9. Unpaged. Illustrated by Gary Hovland. $16.95. ISBN 0-689-86863-4.

4
March

INTRODUCTION

March is a time to recognize the achievements and contributions of women and to celebrate the arrival of spring. March was proclaimed National Women's History Month in 1987. Children will meet American women of achievement, including two Civil War spies who were known as Ellen Bee, women who made scientific discoveries, and others.

Spring celebrations include Mardi Gras and Carnival, St. Patrick's Day, and the Hindu festival of Holi. Children will travel to Brazil and New Orleans to celebrate Mardi Gras and Carnival. They will meet a leprechaun named Erin Gobragh, who wrote a book of Irish blessings, learn about St. Patrick, and discover the three-day Hindu festival of Holi, which celebrates the spring harvest. Learning Extensions include opportunities to develop conversational skills, to create scrapbooks, to learn Cajun music, and other activities related to language arts, social studies, music, art, and the development of critical thinking and research skills.

4.1 NATIONAL WOMEN'S HISTORY MONTH

National Women's History Month recognizes and celebrates the achievements and contributions of women. National Women's History Month had its origins in International Women's Day, which was observed on March 8 during the 1910s and 1920s. The observance fell by the way and was revived again during the 1960s with the emergence of the women's movement. The women's movement questioned the absence of women in traditional American history books and raised both aspirations and opportunities for women. Women's history emerged during the 1970s when political history expanded to include social history. In 1978, the Education Task Force of the Sonoma County (California) Commission on the Status of Women sponsored the first Women's History Week. In 1981, a joint congressional resolution declared the week of March 8 as National Women's History Week. In 1987, National Women's History Week was expanded to the entire month of March.

Atkins, Jeannine. *Wings and Rockets: The Story of Women in Air and Space.* New York: Farrar, Straus & Giroux, 2003. 197p. Illustrated by Dusan Petricic. $17.00. ISBN 0-374-38450-9.

 CHAPTER BOOK—Nonfiction
 Ages 9–14

Summary

This book tells the stories of Katharine Wright, sister of the Wright brothers who was the first woman to ride in an airplane, and eight women pilots: Blanche Stuart Scott, Bessie Coleman, Amelia Earhart, Jackie Cochran, Ann Baumgartner, Jerrie Cobb, Shannon Lucid, and Eileen Collins. A note from the author, a time line of women's aviation history, annotations about important women in aviation history, a bibliography, and a list of Web sites complete the book.

Booktalk

Perhaps you've heard some of these names: Bessie Coleman, Amelia Earhart, and Jackie Cochran. They were among the first woman pilots. More recent names like Jerrie Cobb, Eileen Collins, and Shannon Lucid are women astronauts. Who are they? What did they do? It's all here in *Wings and Rockets: The Story of Women in Air and Space.*

Learning Extensions (Social Studies, Language Arts)

Have children read and then develop a Readers Theater script based on the stories of the nine women featured in this book. Use the bibliography and Web sites listed in the back of the book to research additional information about women in aviation.

Cheney, Lynne. *A Is for Abigail: An Almanac of American Women.* New York: Simon & Schuster Books for Young Readers, 2003. Unpaged. Illustrated by Robin Preiss Glasser. $16.95. ISBN 0-689-85819-1.

 📖 PICTURE BOOK—Nonfiction
  All Ages

Summary

An alphabet book for all ages celebrates American women and their accomplishments. In some cases, it is the individual, such as Abigail Adams, who is featured. In other cases, the individual and others of like accomplishments, such as Emily Dickinson and other women poets, are featured. In still other cases, groups, such as educators, are featured. Pages are busy with print, illustrations, and running text that borders the page and frames the illustrations. The book ends with an alphabetized list of notes related to the text. This is a charming, engaging book loaded with information.

Booktalk

They're all here—America's first ladies, women who went west, others who went to war, and women who made their names as sports figures, writers, entertainers, and more. Come meet women of today and yesterday who helped make America great!

Learning Extensions (Social Studies, Research Skills, Language Arts)

Plan a reception for America's women of accomplishment. Have each child select a woman to portray. Research and learn about the character and attend the reception as that woman. Encourage children to meet and greet each other, introduce themselves, and engage in conversation as their characters. Take time to develop topics of conversation and to develop conversation skills prior to the reception.

Lyons, Mary E., and Muriel M. Branch. *Dear Ellen Bee: A Civil War Scrapbook of Two Union Spies.* New York: Atheneum Books for Young Readers, 2000. 161p. $17.00. ISBN 0-689-82379-7.

 CHAPTER BOOK—Fiction; African-American
Ages 10–14

Summary

A scrapbook format of journal entries, letters, drawings, and assorted memorabilia tell the story of Elizabeth Van Lew (Miss Bet) and Mary Elizabeth Bowser (Liza), one a southern lady, the other a daughter of her freed slave, and how they served as Union spies using the name Ellen Bee during the Civil War. The epilogue and the "About the Text" and "About the Illustrations" sections at the end of the book elaborate on the included documentation.

Booktalk

It all started when one of the prisoners slipped a note into the binding of a book that Miss Bet had taken to the prison. The note said that the New York congressman was taken prisoner and was deathly ill. Miss Bet decided to nurse him back to health. That's how it started. By the time it ended, Miss Bet and her friend Liza had become spies!

Learning Extensions (Social Studies, Language Arts, Art, Research Skills)

Read the prologue and Liza's first entry dated January 1, 1899. Ask the children why Aunt Liza put together a scrapbook for her niece Polly. Making scrapbooks has become a popular hobby. Have the children talk about why people like to make scrapbooks. Then encourage the children to use the scrapbook format to tell a story about a historic event. Write journal entries and save or gather artifacts, such as letters, greeting cards, ticket stubs, and pictures, to include in the journal. Suggest that children illustrate or embellish their scrapbook pages with their own drawings.

Morrison, Lillian. *More Spice Than Sugar: Poems About Feisty Females.* Boston: Houghton Mifflin, 2001. Illustrated by Ann Boyajian. $15.00. ISBN 0-618-06892-9.

 POETRY
 Ages 8–12

Summary

This is an anthology of poems by contemporary poets about spunky girls and women, some real, others not. Black-and-white drawings enliven the pages.

Booktalk/Read-Aloud

You are about to meet an exciting group of women. Some of them are real, like sports figures Aurelia Dobre and Babe Zaharias. Others are just for fun, like Isabel, who ate the bear, and Lucky Sukey, who can run like the wind. Select a poem to read aloud, such as "Love Letter" (written by Delilah telling Samson that his hair is in the jar by the pear tree).

Learning Extensions (Language Arts)

Have the children read, select poems, and read aloud to the whole group. Encourage meaningful animation and expression. Allow time for the children to practice reading aloud before sharing with the group.

Thimmesh, Catherine. *The Sky's the Limit: Stories of Discovery by Women and Girls.* Boston: Houghton Mifflin, 2002. 73p. Illustrated by Melissa Sweet. $16.00. ISBN 0-618-07698-0.

 CHAPTER BOOK—Nonfiction
 Ages 10–14

Summary

Eleven women such as Jane Goodall and Mary Leakey who made notable scientific discoveries are featured. The introduction briefly summarizes the achievements of six other women such as Marie Curie. Finally, a time line from 1300 to 2000 identifies the contributions of another 71 women. The book ends by issuing a challenge to readers to develop their own curiosity. Science fair projects prepared by girls, Web sites, and sources of more information are included.

Booktalk

What do Beatrix Potter, Jane Goodall, and Mary Anning have in common? (Allow time for and encourage student responses.) All three are women who made scientific discoveries. You can meet them and other women who made scientific discoveries—astronomers, archaeologists, and even children—in *The Sky's the Limit*.

Learning Extensions (Social Studies, Language Arts, Research Skills)

Have each child select a woman to research and report on that woman's contribution. Select women featured in the book, identified in the time line, or featured and identified in the books listed next.

Other Books to Use for National Women's History Month

Gormley, Beatrice. *Maria Mitchell: The Soul of an Astronomer.* Grand Rapids, Mich.: Eerdmans Books for Young Readers, 2004. Ages 10–14. 137p. $12.00. ISBN 0-8028-5264-5.

Lyon, George Ella. *Mother to Tigers.* New York: Atheneum Books for Young Readers, 2003. Ages 5–8. Unpaged. Illustrated by Peter Catalanotto. $16.95. ISBN 0-689-84221-X.

Thimmesh, Catherine. *Girls Think of Everything: Stories of Ingenious Inventions by Women.* Boston: Houghton Mifflin, 2000. Ages 8–12. 59p. Illustrated by Melissa Sweet. $6.95. ISBN 0-618-19563-7.

4.2 MARDI GRAS AND CARNIVAL

The celebration of Carnival originated in Rome during the middle of the second century when the 40 days of Lenten fast was preceded by several days of feasting and revelry. Carnival became the Christian celebration of the Roman pagan celebration of Saturnalia and spread from Rome to Europe and America. The New Orleans Mardi Gras was first celebrated in 1827 and is based on the Paris celebration. The name "Mardi Gras: is French, meaning "fat Tuesday." Carnival and Mardi Gras are celebrated with feasts, parades, costumes, and revelry.

Ancona, George. *Carnival.* **New York: Harcourt Brace, 1999. Unpaged. $9.00. ISBN 0-15-201792-5.**

 PICTURE BOOK—Nonfiction; Brazil
Ages 7–12

Summary

Color photos and short text depict the preparation for and celebration of Carnival in Olinda, Brazil.

Bookwalk

It is Carnival! The people of Olinda, Brazil, are preparing to celebrate. The children and teenagers are practicing their songs and dances.

Learning Extensions (Social Skills, Research Skills)

Begin with reading the note from the author. Then have the children research and report on the history of Carnival, its origins in Europe, and celebrations in the Caribbean, Latin America, and New Orleans.

Coil, Suzanne M. *Mardi Gras!* **New York: Macmillan, 1994. 48p. Photographs by Mitchel Osborne. $15.95. ISBN 0-02-722805-3.**

 PICTURE BOOK—Nonfiction
Ages 9–14

Summary

Color photographs and expository text explain Mardi Gras, its history, and the New Orleans celebration with parades, krewes, parties, costumes, and masks.

Booktalk

What is Mardi Gras? Where is it celebrated? How did it begin? What are the krewes—Rex, Bacchus, Endymion, and Zulu? Do you want to know? It's all here, along with parades and music!

Learning Extensions (Social Studies, Critical Thinking Skills)

Use this book and *Carnaval* by George Ancona to compare and contrast the celebrations of Mardi Gras in New Orleans and Carnival in Brazil.

Hoyt-Goldsmith, Diane. *Mardi Gras: A Cajun Country Celebration.* New York: Holiday House, 1995. 32p. Photographs by Lawrence Migdale. $15.95. ISBN 0-8234-1184-2.

 PICTURE BOOK—Nonfiction
 Ages 9–14

Summary

Joel and his family celebrate Mardi Gras in the Cajun bayou country of Eunice, Louisiana. A brief history of the Cajuns and then of Mardi Gras introduces the music, food, games, and celebrations.

Booktalk

It's Mardi Gras, and Joel and his family are celebrating! The costumes and masks are ready. Soon they'll get out the fiddles, accordions, and harmonicas, even the washboards and spoons. It's time for music! Gumbo's cooking, and crawfish are boiling. Everyone's getting hungry. Soon it will be time to eat—but not until after the "run." Join Joel and his family and celebrate Cajun style!

Learning Extensions (Music, Research Skills)

Have the children plan a Cajun-style Mardi Gras celebration by making fringed costumes and masks. Play Zydeco music. Learn the song "La Danse de Mardi Gras" on page 25. Look for Cajun music, such as *A Tribute to Cajun Music* or *Cajun Heat Zydeco Band* in the library collection or on the Internet. Some children might want to research Joel's favorite Cajun musicians mentioned on page 32: Dennis McGee, Dewey Balfa, Wade Fruge, Michael Doucet, and

Ken Smith. Look for their music. Use the recipe on page 18 to make and serve gumbo over rice topped with green onions and served with baked sweet potatoes on the side.

Shaik, Fatima. *On Mardi Gras Day.* New York: Dial Books for Young Readers, 1999. Illustrated by Floyd Cooper. $16.99. ISBN 0-8037-1442-4.

 📖 PICTURE BOOK—Fiction; African-American
 Ages 5–8

Summary

Two African-American children who live in New Orleans wake up bright and early to celebrate Mardi Gras. They dress as deep-sea divers, join the Indians in their dance, and watch the Zulu parade and then the Rex parade. After lunch and a nap, the children play with their friends, then watch the night parade with Papa. An author's note describes and explains the Mardi Gras celebrations.

Read-Aloud

The rich, warm illustrations and simple, lyrical text beg to be seen and heard. Read aloud and show the pictures.

Learning Extensions (Art)

Discuss with the children what images they saw in the book. List the images on the board. Then encourage them to draw and color their own images of Mardi Gras using pastels.

Other Books to Use for Mardi Gras

Landau, Elaine. *Mardi Gras—Parades: Music, Parades and Costumes.* New York: Enslow Publishers, 2002. Ages 4–8. 48p. $23.93. ISBN 0-766-017761.

Rice, James. *Gaston Goes to Mardi Gras.* 2d ed. Gretna, La.: Pelican Publishing, 2000. Ages 4–8. 32p. $15.95. ISBN 1-565-54286-X.

4.3 ST. PATRICK'S DAY

St. Patrick, who introduced Christianity to Ireland in the fifth century, died on March 17, 461. March 17 became the feast of St. Patrick and originally was a Roman Catholic holy day. St. Patrick's

Day has become more of a secular holiday and was first celebrated in America in Boston in 1737. Today, St. Patrick's Day is celebrated with parades, music, green beer, and goodwill to all things Irish.

Freeman, Dorothy Rhodes. *St. Patrick's Day.* Hillside, N.J.: Enslow Publishers, 1992. 48p. $23.93. ISBN 0-89490-383-7.

 📖   CHAPTER BOOK—Nonfiction
  Ages 8–12

Summary

This book tells the story of St. Patrick's life, differentiates between fact and legend, and describes the origin of the holiday and ways that it is celebrated.

Booktalk

Do you think that St. Patrick was Irish? He wasn't. He was a Roman citizen, born in Britain. When he was 16 years old, he was kidnapped by raiders, taken to Ireland, and sold as a slave to an Irish chief. Six years later, he ran away, looking for a ship that would take him home. But that wasn't so easy. Runaway slaves were killed, and people who helped them were punished. Did he ever make it? And why do we call him St. Patrick?

Learning Extensions (Social Studies, Research Skills)

Have some children research Irish history at the time of St. Patrick. Was slavery common? What or who were the Irish chiefs? Have others research the Irish in America. Why did they come to America? Where did they settle? What did they do?

Gobragh, Erin. *Leprechaun Luck: A Wee Book of Irish Wisdom.* New York: Simon & Schuster Books for Young Readers, 2003. Unpaged. Illustrated by Catharine O'Neill. $8.95. ISBN 0-689-85558-3.

 📖   POETRY
  All Ages

Summary

Thirty-eight Irish blessings, each with a cartoonlike illustration, appear one per page. Some are short one-liners, such as "May the hinges of our friendship never grow rusty." Others run as many as 12 lines that fill the entire page. The lilting blessings beg to be heard, while the charming illustrations beg to be seen.

Booktalk/Read-Aloud

A leprechaun wrote this book. His name is Erin Gobragh. (Show the picture of the little old man on the cover.) This is a leprechaun. What kind of a book do you suppose a leprechaun would write? (Have children guess, then read a selection.)

Learning Extensions (Language Arts)

Responses appropriate to this book would be reading aloud by individual children or choral readings, writing new words of wisdom modeled after the book, or creating new illustrations for the verses.

Landau, Elaine. *St. Patrick's Day: Parades, Shamrocks, and Leprechauns.* Berkeley Heights, N.J.: Enslow Publishers, 2002. $23.93. 48p. ISBN 0-7660-1777-X.

　CHAPTER BOOK—Nonfiction
　Ages 7–12

Summary

Five chapters with colored photographs and a map tell the story of St. Patrick's life and describe the celebrations that honor him. Directions for making a leprechaun's pot of gold, a glossary, suggestions for further reading, and Internet addresses complete the book.

Booktalk

Leprechauns, shamrocks, the color green, corned beef, and cabbage are all part of a St. Patrick's Day celebration. But who was St. Patrick, and what made him special to Ireland?

Learning Extensions (Language Arts)

Have the children plan a puppet show that retells the story of St. Patrick's life. Write a script, make puppets, and assign roles.

Then divide the children into three groups. Let each group choose a project for your celebration. Use the book for ideas. Have one group make decorations, such as shamrocks, hats, and harps. Have the children use the instructions in the back of the book to make a leprechaun's pot of gold. Have another group plan, prepare, and serve refreshments, such as green Jell-O cupcakes or sugar cookies with green icing, and green lemonade. Have the third group select Irish music, such as "When Irish Eyes Are Smiling," "Too-Ra-Loo-Ra-Loo-Ra," and "My Wild Irish Rose," to play or sing. Prepare invitations and invite families and friends to your celebration.

MacGill-Callahan, Sheila. *The Last Snake in Ireland: A Story About St. Patrick.* New York: Holiday House, 1999. Unpaged. Illustrated by Will Hillenbrand. $15.45. ISBN 0-8234-1425-6.

 PICTURE BOOK—Fiction
 Ages 5–9

Summary

This is a fun elaboration on the legend of St. Patrick driving the snakes from Ireland. Cartoonlike illustrations add to the humor of the book. In this story, St. Patrick drives all the snakes out of Ireland except one big old red snake that eventually lands in Loch Ness, Scotland, and becomes the Loch Ness Monster.

Booktalk

It was easy driving the snakes out of Ireland until St. Patrick discovered one big old red snake wrapped in the bushes. It was the Loch Ness Monster! That's when St. Patrick's work really began!

Learning Extensions (Research Skills)

Form two groups. Use this book as a springboard for one group to research other accounts of the legend of St. Patrick driving the snakes from Ireland. Have the second group research accounts of the mystery of the Loch Ness Monster. A third group might want to research snakes—their characteristics, behavior, habitat, and so on—and then illustrate a report with a drawing of a snake.

66 ■ *March*

Other Books to Use for St. Patrick's Day

Gomez, Rebecca. *It's St. Patrick's Day!* New York: Scholastic Readers, 2004. Ages 3–6. 32p. $3.99. ISBN 0-439-44160-9.

Heaney, Marie. *The Names upon the Harp: Irish Myth and Legend.* New York: Arthur A. Levine Books, 2000. All ages. 96p. Illustrated by P. J. Lynch. $19.95. ISBN 0-590-68052-8.

Tompert, Ann. *Saint Patrick.* Honesdale, Pa.: Boyds Mills Press, 2005. Ages 4–8. 32p. Illustrated by Michael Garland. $8.95. ISBN 1-56397-992-6.

4.4 HOLI

Holi is the three-day Hindu festival of colors that celebrates the spring harvest. It falls on the full-moon day in the month of Phalgun in the Hindu calendar and corresponds with the month of March in the Gregorian calendar. Mythological origins vary, but Holi is first mentioned as an ancient Aryan festival in old Sanskrit texts. Holi is celebrated with bonfires, music, singing, dancing, plays, and throwing colored water into the air. Everyone places ashes from the bonfires on their foreheads.

Kadodwala, Dilip. *Holi.* Austin, Tex.: Raintree Steck-Vaughn, 1997. 30p. $27.79. ISBN 0-8172-4610-X.

 📖 PICTURE BOOK—Nonfiction; Hindu
 Ages 7–12

Summary

Color photographs and short paragraphs briefly explain Hinduism and the holiday of Holi, present stories associated with the holiday, and describe its celebration. Directions for making an elephant mask and a recipe for making a sweet dessert conclude the book with a glossary and suggestions for further reading.

Booktalk

Have you ever played a practical joke? Has anyone played a practical joke on you? What would happen if you dumped colored water on someone or smeared colored powder on your father's face? You might be surprised to hear that this is how some children celebrate a holiday. Hindu children and their families think this is a fun way to remember the tricks that their god, Krishna, likes to play. You can find out more about this holiday and the stories behind it in *Holi.*

Learning Extensions (Social Studies, Language Arts, Art)

Have the children use the suggestions for further reading in the back of the book to learn more about India, Hinduism, and the holiday of Holi. Some may want to read and retell Hindu stories, such as those retold in Debjani Chatterjee's *The Elephant-Headed God and Other Hindu Tales.* Use the directions on page 28 to make elephant masks.

Other Books to Use for Holi

Krishnaswami, Uma. *Holi.* New York: Childrens Press, 2003. Ages 4–8. 32p. $5.95. ISBN 0-516-277642.

Pandya, Meenal. *Here Comes Holi: The Festival of Colors.* Wellesley, Mass.: MeeRa Publications, 2003. Ages 4–8. 32p. $14.94. ISBN 0-963-553941.

5
April

INTRODUCTION

April is National Poetry Month. Celebrate by inviting families to a coffeehouse to listen to poetry readings. Celebrate African-American experiences, Amish life, homes across America, and poems from the Middle East.

The return of spring brings the celebrations of Passover and Easter and the observance of Earth Day. Join Micah and Pearl as they celebrate Passover with their families. Travel with Moses and the Hebrews as they escape from Egypt and travel through the wilderness to the Promised Land. Meet Nibbles O'Hare, who told the rabbits that he was the Easter Bunny. Re-read the Easter story and enter into a little girl's dream. Then travel to Israel, learn how it was covered with trees, reduced to a desert, and restored to a fertile land. Meet young people who are making a difference in today's world by helping to protect and heal the environment. Learn about trees of the world, and, finally, celebrate the environment with Ms. Webster and her class. Suggested learning activities include creating and presenting a Readers Theater, making and then acting out with finger puppets, art activities, character education, and service learning projects.

5.1 NATIONAL POETRY MONTH

In 1996, the Academy of American Poets declared April National Poetry Month. This is a time to celebrate poetry with readings, festivals, book displays, and workshops. The Academy of American Poets creates and distributes National Poetry Month posters that are mailed free to teachers, librarians, and booksellers on request.

Bryan, Ashley. *Ashley Bryan's ABC of African American Poetry.* New York: Aladdin Paperbacks, 2001. Unpaged. $5.99. ISBN 0-689-84045-4.

  PICTURE BOOK—Poetry; African-American
  Ages 5 and up

Summary

Bold and brilliantly colored full-page illustrations illuminate this collection of poetry that celebrates African-American experiences.

Read-Aloud

Show the title page so that children can see the illustrations and again read the title. Begin with the letter A. Read aloud and show the illustration. Continue by reading aloud and showing the illustrations of three or five more letters of your choosing, possibly using initials of some of the children. Be sure to read the poetry with expression and feeling.

Learning Extensions (Language Arts)

Have children write their names in big letters. Have them choose a feeling and an image they would like to portray and write and illustrate poems on the basis of those feelings and images.

High, Linda Oatman. *A Humble Life: Plain Poems.* Grand Rapids, Mich.: Eerdmans Books for Young Readers, 2001. Unpaged. Illustrated by Bill Farnsworth. $17.00. ISBN 0-8028-5207-6.

  PICTURE BOOK—Poetry; Amish
  Ages 5 and up

Summary

A collection of poems celebrates a year in the lives of the Amish and the Mennonite, also known as the Plain People.

Read-Aloud

Choose a poem such as "Come Spring," "Thanksgiving Dinner," or "Shivery Winter Mornings" and read aloud.

Learning Extensions (Language Arts)

Free verse using specific details creates the powerful images in these poems. Tell the children to close their eyes and listen for specific details while you re-read the poem. Ask children to share the details that they heard. Then talk about the experiences that the children have with the topic of the poem, such as spring, Thanksgiving, or winter. List specific details, then ask the children to compose their own group poem with those details.

Hopkins, Lee Bennett. *Home to Me: Poems Across America.* New York: Orchard Books, 2002. 44p. Illustrated by Stephen Alcorn. $17.95. ISBN 0-439-34096-9.

 PICTURE BOOK—Poetry
 Ages 8–12

Summary

An anthology of poems by authors such as Jane Yolen, Joseph Bruchac, Tony Johnson, and others describes home—home on a lake, on a reservation, on a dairy farm, and other diverse places across our country.

Bookwalk

This is a book about homes. Turn the pages of the book and name the home that each poem is about. The illustrations alone will encourage the children to read the poems.

Learning Extensions (Language Arts)

The poems in this book lend themselves to choral readings. There are 15 poems, 14 of which are written in stanzas. The simplest choral reading pattern is to divide your group into two smaller groups and have them alternate reading the stanzas. Another approach would be to form one small group for each stanza and have each group read a stanza. For a poem such as "First Saturday Morning: Beaumont, Texas," which has 13 two-line stanzas, select 13 children to each read a stanza. For the poem "Wildwood By-the-Sea," have a group read the first two lines of the stanza, one child read the third line, a second child read lines 4 and 5, a third child read lines 6 and 7, and a fourth child read lines 8 and 9 to complete the stanza. Repeat the pattern for each of the following stanzas. Finally, encourage your children to create their own grouping patterns.

Extend the book and activity by gathering a collection of poetry anthologies by Lee Bennett Hopkins. Encourage children to select a poem and then have them read aloud or recite the poem individually or in groups. Provide time for them to practice their public speaking skills before reading or reciting to the group.

Nye, Naomi Shihab. *The Flag of Childhood: Poems from the Middle East.* New York: Aladdin Paperbacks, 2002. 99p. $3.99. ISBN 0-689-85172-3.

 ANTHOLOGY—Poetry; Middle East
 Ages 8–12

Summary

This is an anthology of poems by contemporary writers from Palestine, Israel, Egypt, Iraq, Turkey, Tunisia, Lebanon, Jordan, Iran, Saudi Arabia, Yemen, Bahrain, Morocco, and Syria. Naomi Shihab Nye has organized the writings of contemporary poets about contemporary tensions around the chapter titles "A Galaxy of Seeds," "The World Is a Glass You Drink From," " Pick a Sky and Name It," and "There Was in Our House a River."

Read-Aloud

Introduce this collection of thought-provoking poems by reading aloud or reciting short, simple poems, such as "Poem," "Talk," or "The Bridge."

Learning Extensions (Language Arts, Social Studies, Critical Thinking)

Some poems are powerful and clear, others obscure and thought provoking. Read the entire collection before using with students. Select poems appropriate to stimulate thinking and discussion. All are timely to use in conjunction with current world events involving the Middle East. Immigrant students from the Middle East will relate to the poems, as will students whose families are from the Middle East.

Other Books to Use for National Poetry Month

Levy, Constance. *Splash! Poems of Our Watery World.* New York: Orchard Books, 2002. Ages 8–12. 48p. Illustrated by David Soman. $16.95. ISBN 0-43-29318-9.

Sidman, Joyce. *Song of the Water Boatman.* Boston: Houghton Mifflin, 2005. Ages 8–12. Unpaged. Illustrated by Beckie Prange. $16.00. ISBN 0-618-13547-2.

Singer, Marilyn. *Fireflies at Midnight.* New York: Atheneum, 2003. Ages 5–9. Unpaged. Illustrated by Ken Robbins. $16.95. ISBN 0-689-82492-0.

5.2 PASSOVER

Passover is an eight-day observance that commemorates the Exodus—the flight from Egypt by the Israelites during the reign of Pharaoh Ramses II. Passover begins on the fifteenth day of the Jewish month of Nissan and falls in either March or April of the Gregorian calendar. Passover begins with a meal called Seder, a formal meal of special foods and rituals. The family gathers for Seder and during the meal retells the story of the flight from Egypt.

Hoyt-Goldsmith, Diane. *Celebrating Passover.* New York: Holiday House, 2000. 32p. Photographs by Lawrence Migdale. $16.95. ISBN 0-8234-1429-5.

    PICTURE BOOK—Nonfiction
    Ages 9–12

Summary

Micah and his family prepare for and celebrate Passover by cleaning, shopping, cooking, and finally by sitting down to the Seder. The book begins with the story of Passover and an explanation of the Haggadah and the foods of Passover. A two-page spread features the Seder plate and the symbols of Passover. A recipe for haroset, Hebrew words and music for the song "Dayenu," a glossary, and an index are included.

Booktalk

The youngest child asks, "Why is this night different from all other nights?" On this night, the meal is a ceremony of readings, prayers, and singing and the eating of special foods. Micah's family prepares for Passover by cleaning, shopping, cooking, and dressing in their best clothes. What is so special about this night? What is Passover, and why is it celebrated around the world?

Learning Extensions (Language Arts)

Let children respond to the questions raised in the Booktalk by sharing what they know about Passover. Then show the two-page spread on pages 18 and 19. Retell the Passover story by explaining the significance of the symbols on page 19. Conclude by having the children make haroset using the recipe on page 10. Then serve haroset on matza bread and let the children eat it.

Marx, David F. *Passover.* New York: Childrens Press, 2001. 32p. ISBN 0-516-22214-7.

 PICTURE BOOK—Nonfiction
 Ages 5–7

Summary

Photographs and simple text explain the history and celebration of Passover.

Read-Aloud

The short, simple text and full-page photographs lend themselves to reading aloud and showing the photographs.

Learning Extensions (Language Arts)

Show the pictures to the children and ask them to retell what is happening in each picture. Have children create a storyboard or book about their own favorite holiday.

Wildsmith, Brian. *Exodus*. Grand Rapids, Mich.: Eerdmans Book for Young Readers, 1999. Unpaged. $20.00. ISBN 0-8028-5175-4.

    PICTURE BOOK—Nonfiction; Old Testament; Jewish; Christian

All Ages

Summary

The story of Moses and the Hebrews, the first Passover, their escape from Egypt, and their journey through the wilderness to the Promised Land is told. Finely detailed illustrations and gold tone–bordered pages supplement the text. This book is likely to be welcomed by church groups, Christian schools, parents who homeschool, and family and friends who are looking for books that retell the Bible stories for young people.

Bookwalk

Retell the story by showing the pictures and focusing on the details in the pictures. Finely detailed illustrations with particular attention to the architecture of the time and place are of particular note.

Learning Extensions (Art, Social Studies)

Have students select and illustrate one event in the story using colored markers or crayons. Art teachers might want to use the illustrations in this book as a model for representing depth and perspective as in the long line of people traveling through the wilderness and as a model showing intricate details, such as the feathering of the birds, striations on the rocks, and fingers of flame. A map activity would also be appropriate. Have children trace the journey on a map and research the climate of the countries. What types of problems might be encountered on such a journey?

Zalben, Jane Breskin. *Pearl's Passover: A Family Celebration Through Stories, Recipes, Crafts, and Songs*. New York: Simon & Schuster Books for Young Readers. 2002. Unpaged. $16.00. ISBN 0-689-81487-9.

📖 PICTURE BOOK—Fiction; Nonfiction
Ages 3–9

Summary

Pearl and her family are preparing to celebrate Passover. Directions for craft items, food recipes, Passover songs, blessings in English and Hebrew, a map showing the Exodus from Egypt, information about the 10 Plagues, the 15 Steps of the Seder, the Four Questions, and the biblical story of the first Passover are interspersed with the fictional story of Pearl and her family. A glossary appears at the end of the book.

Booktalk

The family gathers. Cousin Harry wants to find the afikomen. Grandpa says we have to take the chametz to the synagogue. Avi will ask the Four Questions. Mam says we still have much to do before tonight's Seder. Finally, the guests arrive. Aunt Rachel says, "Shh," and we're ready to begin.

Learning Extensions (Art, Language Arts)

Use the directions on page 26. Have the children make finger puppets. Then act out the Passover story on pages 18 to 19.

Other Books to Use for Passover

Chevat, Richie. *A Pickles Passover.* New York: Simon Spotlight/Nickelodeon, 2003. Ages 5–7. Unpaged. $3.50. ISBN 0-689-85232-0.

Kimmel, Eric A. *A Passover Companion: Wonders and Miracles.* New York: Scholastic, 2004. All ages. 23p. $18.95. ISBN 0-439-07175-5.

Sper, Emily. *The Passover Seder.* New York: Cartwheel Books, 2003. Ages 3–6. 12p. $9.95. ISBN 0-439-44312-1.

5.3 EASTER

Easter is a movable feast that falls on the first Sunday following the full moon that occurs on or following the spring equinox (March 21). The earliest that Easter can occur is on March 22, the latest on April 25. Originally, Easter was a pagan festival observed by the ancient Saxons who celebrated the return of spring. In the second century, Easter became a Christian feast commemorating the resurrection of Jesus Christ.

Paraskevas, Betty, and Michael Paraskevas. *Nibbles O'Hare.* New York: Simon & Schuster Books for Young Readers, 2001. Unpaged. $16.00. ISBN 0-689-82865-9.

 PICTURE BOOK—Fiction
 Ages 4–8

Summary

Nibbles tells the other rabbits that he is the Easter Bunny when, in truth, he is "wanted" for stealing produce. When One-Eyed Jack finds the old "Wanted" poster and tells the rabbits the truth, they all turn on Nibbles and refuse to deliver the Easter eggs. However, Nibbles wins the respect of the rabbits by working alone all night long.

Booktalk

Nibbles the rabbit has a habit of getting into trouble. He is wanted for stealing produce and has to get out of town. Nibbles and his friend Struts find an abandoned playhouse on the grounds of an abandoned mansion. With the help of their new friend, Wacky Shellhammer, they fix it up and move in. All the rabbits in the neighborhood are jealous when they see the fine home that Nibbles, Struts, and Wacky have made.. What does Nibbles do? He lies to the rabbits and tells them he is the Easter Bunny. Now everyone loves Nibbles—until Easter draws near. Oh, oh! Nibbles is in trouble again!

Learning Extensions (Character Education)

Use this book to develop a discussion that centers on the consequences of one's behavior. Begin with book related questions. Nibbles steals produce and later lies about it. What are the consequences of those behaviors? Nibbles repairs the playhouse and works all night to deliver the Easter eggs. What are the consequences of those behaviors? Diagram Nibbles's behaviors and consequences. Extend the discussion to children's behaviors in the library, at school, at home, or in the neighborhood. Help the children identify the consequences of their behaviors. Use this book in conjunction with your character education program focusing on "honesty" or "responsibility."

Thompson, Lauren. *Love One Another: The Story of Easter.* New York: Scholastic, 2000. Unpaged. Illustrated by Elizabeth Uyehara. $15.95. ISBN 0-590-31830-6.

 📖 PICTURE BOOK—Nonfiction; Christian
 Ages 3 and up

Summary

Bold, brilliantly colored oil-on-canvas illustrations supplement the retelling of the Easter Story. Three dramatic two-page spreads highlight the raising of Jesus on the cross, his last words, and finally his death. Based on the gospels of Mathew, Mark, Luke, and John, this book is likely to be welcomed by church groups, Christian schools, parents who homeschool, and family and friends who are looking for books that retell the gospel stories for young people.

Booktalk

Crowds cheer when Jesus enters the city of Jerusalem. But the priests are angry, and they plot to arrest him. Do you know what happens next? There's a happy ending to a sad story.

Learning Extensions (Language Arts)

Begin by showing the book and asking children to retell what they know about the Easter story. Read aloud and show the pictures. The final messages of the book are to love one another, to know that wrongs are forgiven, and that love is greater than hate. Engage children in a discussion of what these messages mean in their lives.

Tudor, Tasha. *A Tale for Easter.* New York: Simon & Schuster Books for Young Readers, 2001. Unpaged. $12.95. ISBN 0-689-82844-6.

 📖 PICTURE BOOK—Fiction
 All Ages

Summary

This reissue of Tasha Tudor's charming tale about a little girl's Easter Eve dream tells of riding the back of a fawn to discover the rabbits and mice, lambs and ducklings, and bluebirds and robins of early spring.

Read-Aloud

Share the charm of Tasha Tudor's lilting language and delicate watercolor illustrations by reading aloud and showing the pictures.

Learning Extensions (Art)

After reading aloud, have children make pictures of the signs of spring and signs of Easter. Provide children with watercolors for painting or have them make thumbprint pictures using colored ink pads and felt markers.

Wildsmith, Brian. *The Easter Story.* Grand Rapids, Mich.: Eerdmans Books for Young Readers, 2000. 32p. $18.00. ISBN 0-80208-5189-4.

📖 PICTURE BOOK—Christian
All Ages

Summary

The donkey that Jesus rode into the city of Jerusalem on Palm Sunday becomes a main character in this retelling of the Easter story. Rich gold tones illuminate finely detailed illustrations that include at least one angel on every page. This book is likely to be welcomed by church groups, Christian schools, families that homeschool, and family and friends who are looking for books that retell the gospel stories for young people.

Booktalk/Bookwalk/Read-Aloud

The donkey Jesus rode into Jerusalem has a story to tell. It was an amazing day. Crowds gathered and cried out, "Hosanna!" They even spread out their clothes and palm branches to walk on. Read aloud and show the pictures or retell the story by showing the pictures. Be sure to focus on the details in the pictures. Finely detailed illustrations with particular attention to the architecture of the time and place are of particular note.

Learning Extensions (Language Arts)

Have children think of a familiar story they know and retell it from a different perspective. For example, retell the story Goldilocks and the Three Bears from Baby Bear's perspective or the story of George Washington and the cherry tree from his mother's perspective.

Other Books to Use for Easter

Grimes, Nikki. *At Jerusalem's Gate: Poems of Easter.* Grand Rapids, Mich.: Eerdmans Books for Young Readers, 2005. All ages. 48p. Illustrated by David Frampton. $20.00. ISBN 0-8028-5183-5.

Samuel, Catherine. *Timmy's Eggs-Ray Vision.* New York: Simon & Schuster, 2005. Ages 4–8. 16p. Illustrated by Zina Saunders. $5.00. ISBN 0-689-87229-1.

Zolotow, Charlotte. *The Bunny Who Found Easter.* Boston: Houghton Mifflin, 1959, 1987, 1998. Ages 4–8. Unpaged. $5.95. ISBN 0-618-11127-1.

5.4 EARTH DAY

In 1970, April 22 was proclaimed Earth Day. The purpose of Earth Day is to recognize and respect the Earth's system of balance and to promote awareness that people's actions can preserve or destroy that balance.

Alexander, Sue, and Leonid Gore. *Behold the Trees.* New York: Arthur A. Levine Books, 2001. Unpaged. $16.95. ISBN 0-590-76211-7.

  PICTURE BOOK—Nonfiction; Israel
  Ages 9 and up

Summary

This book begins in 5000 b.c.e. and ends with the present day. It tells the story of the land that is now Israel—how it was once covered with trees, then reduced to a desert and restored to a fertile land with life-sustaining vegetation. The almost mystical quality of the illustrations and text begs to be seen and heard.

Read-Aloud

Read aloud and show the illustrations.

Learning Extensions (Language Arts, Social Studies, Science, Research Skills, Service Learning)

Read aloud the author's note. Ask children what they know about Arbor Day and Earth Day. Research the origins and purposes of these observances. Discuss and decide on a project that your group can complete for this year's observance.

Hoose, Phillip. "Healing the Earth." In *It's Our World, Too! Young People Who Are Making a Difference* (pp. 76–100). New York: Farrar, Straus & Giroux, 2002. 166p. $13.00. ISBN 0-374-33622-9.

 📖 CHAPTER BOOK—Nonfiction
  Ages 9–14

Summary

This book describes how young people are making a difference in today's world. In particular, "Healing the Earth" tells of young people who make a difference by protecting the natural environment. The second half of the book, "A Handbook for Young Activists," tells how to get started and what tools to use.

Booktalk

Twelve-year-old Andrew Holleman studies the law books at the public library, then circulates a petition to prevent a land developer from destroying a forest in Massachusetts. First-and second-grade Swedish students buy part of a rain forest in Costa Rica and establish the Children's Rain Forest. Fifteen-year-old Joel Rubin saves the dolphins from being killed by tuna fishermen when he organizes his classmates to write and mail postcards to the executives of Heinz, Bumble Bee, and Van Camp. Young people around the world are making a difference, and so can you! How might you make a difference? Find out how to get started and what tools you need to effect change.

Learning Extensions (Service Learning)

Use these selections to promote service learning projects. Encourage students to take action and to provide guidance as to how to make a difference. If students do not have a project that they wish to pursue, perhaps they would like to sponsor a fund-raiser and contribute the proceeds to the Children's Rain Forest fund. For more information, see pages 92 and 93. Also check the resources at the back of the book.

McDonnell, Janet. *Celebrating Earth Day.* Chicago: Childrens Press, 1994. 31p. Illustrated by Diana Magnuson. $4.99. ISBN 0-516-00689-4.

 PICTURE BOOK—Fiction
Ages 7–10

Summary

Ms. Webster teaches her class about Earth Day. She and her students clean up the bike path, recycle cans and bottles, shop for things that make less rather than more garbage, make posters, invite parents to a party, and plant a tree. The book ends with four pages of suggested activities.

Booktalk

Ms. Webster and her class make posters about recycling, saving water, keeping the air clean, and "shopping the Earth Day way." How do you celebrate Earth Day?

Learning Extensions (Language Arts, Science, Art)

After reading the book, brainstorm with your children ways in which you can avoid litter, recycle, "shop the Earth Day way," conserve water, and keep the air clean. Appoint a recorder to record on the chalkboard, whiteboard, or chart paper the children's ideas. Have the children organize their ideas into lists, then make posters. Extend the activity by planning an Earth Day party as did the children in the book. Create and send invitations to families and friends, "shop the Earth Day way" for refreshments, and decorate with the children's posters. Play "pin the trash on the garbage can" and present a program that shares what you have learned about Earth Day.

Miller, Debbie S. *Are Trees Alive?* New York: Walker & Co., 2002. 32p. Illustrated by Stacey Schuett. $16.95. ISBN 0-8027-88-1-7.

■ *April*

📖 PICTURE BOOK—Nonfiction; Multicultural
Ages 3–7

Summary

Multicultural illustrations featuring African, Native American, Indian, Asian, Caucasian, and Hispanic children and adults augment simple text that provides basic information about trees. Illustrations on the last three pages accompany information about trees of the world.

Bookwalk

As you turn the pages, point out the important features. Trees are awesome! Just look! Roots, trunks, branches, and bark each play an important role in the life of a tree. The crown provides shade, leaves breath, and sap travels between the roots and the leaves. Trees grow flowers and seeds. Some trees die. Some lose their leaves. Others blossom. Conclude with a discussion of the last page. How can the forest have a picnic? Call attention to the information about trees on the last three pages of the book.

Learning Extensions (Service Learning)

The author suggests planting a tree after reading this book. She invites readers to send digital pictures of their trees to her Web site at www.debbiemillaralaska.com. She also suggests visiting the National Arbor Day Foundation's Web site at www.arborday.org for more information about planting trees in your state.

Other Books to Use for Earth Day

Bourgeois, Paulette, and Brenda Clark. *Franklin Plants a Tree.* New York: Scholastic, 2001. Ages 4–7. 32p. $4.50. ISBN 0-439-20382-1.

Drawson, Blair. *Mary Margaret's Tree.* New York: Orchard Books, 1996. Ages 4–7. 40p. $15.95. ISBN 0-531-09521-5.

Morrison, Gordon. *Oak Tree.* Boston: Houghton Mifflin, 2000. Ages 5–12. 30p. $16.00. ISBN 0-395-95644-7.

6
May

INTRODUCTION

May is National Asian/Pacific Heritage Month, a time to celebrate the accomplishments of many Asian ethnic groups. Children will meet Confucius, a Chinese scholar and thinker; Sondak, the first woman to rule in eastern Asia; and Hokusai, a Japanese painter. A story of ancient Thailand and a contemporary Asian-American story encourage children to find out where their families came from. We also celebrate the Mexican fiesta of Cinco de Mayo, which commemorates the defeat of the French in 1862, and Mother's Day, which originated with the ancient Greeks. Learning extensions include researching hunger and the world food supply, using map skills, and developing a K-W-L (what do we Know, what do we Want to know, and what did we Learn) chart.

Other activities relate to art, music and dance, social studies, language arts, and character education as well as research, critical thinking, and study skills.

6.1 NATIONAL ASIAN/PACIFIC HERITAGE MONTH

May commemorates the arrival of the first Japanese immigrants to the United States in May 1843 and celebrates the accomplishments of many Asian ethnic groups. President Jimmy Carter declared May 4–10, 1979, the first Asian Pacific Heritage Week. In 1990, President George Bush expanded the celebration to the entire month of May. Legislation approved on October 23, 1992, designated May to be National Asian Pacific Heritage Month.

Freedman, Russell. *Confucius: The Golden Rule.* New York: Arthur A. Levine Books, 2002. Unpaged. Illustrated by Frederic Clement. $15.95. ISBN 0-439-13957-0.

 📖 PICTURE BOOK—Nonfiction; Chinese
  Ages 9–14

Summary

This biography of Confucius begins with a brief introduction to his teachings and concludes with the author's note describing the celebration of Confucius' birthday in the city of Qufu near his birth and burial places. A note on sources and suggestions for further reading and a list of sources of quotations from the Analects of Confucius complete the text.

Booktalk

Confucius was a scholar, a teacher, an excellent horseman, and a hunter. He also became a great spiritual leader of the Chinese people. The China in which he lived was in turmoil, with wealthy landowners fighting among themselves. Confucius became governor of a small province and then police commissioner, but because the ruler of the province did not live up to Confucius' moral standards, Confucius resigned. He set out in search for a ruler who would allow him to put into practice his ideas about government. Did he find that ruler? How did Confucius' teachings spread and endure for more than 2,000 years?

Learning Extensions (Social Studies, Character Education, Research Skills)

Include this book in your character education program. The principals and ideals of Confucius have influenced the Western world and are named and elaborated on throughout the book. Engage children in a discussion of those ideals and principals. Discuss why it is important that we each ask, "What is the right thing to do?"

Learn more about Confucius by using the resources suggested in the back of the book as well as on the Internet to conduct research. Type "Confucius," "Kong Fuzi," or "Kung Fu-tzu" into a search engine of your choice. Have children share their findings with the entire group. Conclude with a celebration of Confucius' birthday that includes reading selections from the sayings of Confucius.

Holman, Sheri. *Sondak: Princess of the Moon and Stars.* New York: Scholastic, 2002. 192p. $10.95. ISBN 0-439-16586-5.

 CHAPTER BOOK—Fiction; Korean
 Ages 9–14

Summary

Queen Sondak was the first woman to rule in eastern Asia. She governed ancient Korea during the Three Kingdom period (seventh century). This fictional biography is the story of Sondak, a teenage princess who tested her knowledge of astronomy against the influence of the Chinese ambassador. The book ends with an epilogue; a historical note; Sondak's family tree; other members of the royal family; photographs of artifacts and places; an explanation of Confucianism, Buddhism, and Shamanism; a glossary; information about the author; acknowledgments; and a list of other books in the *Royal Diaries* series.

Booktalk

As a young girl, Princess Sondak learns from her father's astronomers how to recognize the stars and the constellations. When she is 14 years old, the Chinese ambassador visits her father. Sondak challenges the ambassador's calculations that predicted a solar eclipse. This is serious business—a solar eclipse requires certain rituals to call back the sun. If the eclipse does not occur, Sondak's father will be humiliated before his subjects. Who do you think is right?

Learning Extensions (Social Studies)

Ask children if they know where Korea is. Find Korea on a world map or globe, then use the epilogue, historical note, and other information, including pictures, map, and family tree, to learn more about Korea during the time that Sondak lived. Extend the activity by using *Timetables of History: A Horizontal Linkage of People and Events* from Touchstone Press to learn what was happening in the rest of the world during Sondak's lifetime. An activity about solar eclipses is also appropriate here. When was the last one? When will the next one occur? What causes an eclipse, and how often do they occur? What are some of the ancient myths about solar eclipses?

Krudop, Walter Lyon. *The Man Who Caught Fish.* New York: Farrar, Straus & Giroux, 2000. Unpaged. $16.00. ISBN 0-374-34786-7.

 📖 PICTURE BOOK—Fiction; Thailand
  Ages 5 and up

Summary

A stranger with a fishing pole pulls up one fish for one person until the arrogant king demands a basketful of fish. Having broken the stranger's spell, the king becomes the next fisherman to pull up one fish for one person.

Booktalk

A stranger comes to a village and drops his fishing line into the water. He pulls out a fish, gives it to a woman, and says, "One person, one fish." As the fisherman gives fish to the townspeople, word spreads until the king comes to see the fisherman. The king demands a basketful of fish and becomes very angry when the fisherman gives him only one fish. The king offers the fisherman a priceless jade sculpture in exchange for a basketful of fish. But the fisherman just pulls up but one fish saying, "One person, one fish." All of a sudden, the king has an idea! (Stop here. Ask the children what the king's idea might be. Ask them if they think the king will get his basketful of fish. Tell the children that they will have to read the rest of the book to find out.)

Learning Extensions (Social Studies, Research Skills)

This is a story about a greedy king. Begin the discussion about greed by talking about the king, his greed, and the stranger. Ask the children if they think the king and the stranger learned anything about being greedy. Is there a lesson that we can all learn from the king and the stranger? Then extend the discussion to the children's lives. Have they ever been greedy and demanding? What happened? Did they learn anything?

Pak, Soyung. *A Place to Grow.* New York: Arthur A. Levine Books, 2002. Unpaged. Illustrated by Marcelino Truong. $16.95. ISBN 0-439-13015-8.

    📖 PICTURE BOOK—Fiction
       Ages 5 and up

Summary

As a little girl and her father plant a garden, the father tells the little girl what seeds and people need to grow. This book depicts a universal experience using Asian-American characters and illustrations.

Read-Aloud

The lyrical text with brilliant illustrations begs to be read aloud. Hold up the book to show the children and ask them what they think the book might be about. After some predicting, say, "Let's read and find out." Show the pictures as you read the text.

Learning Extensions (Critical Thinking Skills)

After reading aloud, build on the children's predictions. Ask if the book was what they thought it would be. Ask how a garden is like people. What does a garden need to grow? What do people need to grow? Extend the book by asking children to find out where their families came from and why they chose to live in the community they chose.

Ray, Deborah Kogan. *Hokusai: The Man Who Painted a Mountain.* New York: Farrar, Straus & Giroux, 2001. Unpaged. $18.00. ISBN 0-374-33263-0.

 📖 PICTURE BOOK—Nonfiction; Japanese
   Ages 8–12

Summary

Richly detailed illustrations accompany the biographic text telling the life story of the prolific Japanese artist Hokusai. His famous woodcut *The Great Wave off Kanagawa* appears at the end of the book, while endpapers, both front and back, show some of his many sketches.

Booktalk

The artist who changed the art of Japan and even the art of the Western world is known as Hokusai, but Hokusai is only one of the more than 30 names that he used. Tokitaro, meaning firstborn son, was the name his mother gave him. Shunro is one of the first names that he took at the age of 18 to celebrate his new life as an artist. When he shifted to a Chinese style of painting, he changed his name to Sori. He was 36 when he took the name of Hokusai. Much later he called himself Gakyo Rojin, meaning "old man mad about painting." His most famous painting is *The Great Wave off Kanagawa.* (Show the picture at the end of the book.) He produced more than 30,000 pieces of art. Some of his sketches are shown here in the endpapers. (Show front and back endpapers.)

Learning Extensions (Art)

Use this book as a springboard to art appreciation. Display pictures of the "floating world" done in the ukiyo-e style, examples of Hokusai's sketches and paintings, and works by French impressionists such as Manet, Degas, Cassatt, Gauguin, and van Gogh, who were influenced by Hokusai. Have children discuss what they think the artists were trying to "say" or accomplish. Your library collection or nearby art museum may have slides that you and your children can view. Perhaps a nearby art museum has pieces in its collection that you may see. A selected bibliography at the end of the book suggests additional books about Hokusai and his thousands of drawings and paintings.

Other Book to Use for National Asian/Pacific Heritage Month

Demi. *The Emperor's New Clothes.* New York: Margaret K. McElderry Books, 2000. Ages 3 and up. Unpaged. $19.85. ISBN 0-689-83068-8.

Recorvits, Helen. *My Name Is Yoon.* New York: Frances Foster Books, 2003. Ages 7–10. Unpaged. Illustrated by Gabi Swiatkowska. $16.00. ISBN 0-374-35114-7.

Yep, Lawrence. *Lady of Ch'iao Kuo Warrior of the South: Southern China, a.d. 531.* New York: Scholastic, 2001. Ages 8–14. 224p. $10.95. ISBN 0-439-22598-6.

6.2 CINCO DE MAYO

Cinco de Mayo, the fifth of May, commemorates the victory of the Mexicans over the French at the Battle of Pueblo in 1862. The holiday is observed in Mexico and in cities in the United States that have a significant Mexican population. The holiday is a celebration of Mexico's native peoples and their culture, food, music, dance, and customs.

MacMillan, Dianne M. *Mexican Independence Day and Cinco de Mayo.* Springfield, N.J.: Enslow Publishers, 1997. 48p. $23.93. ISBN 0-89490-816-2.

 📖 CHAPTER BOOK—Nonfiction
 Ages 8–12

Summary

Photographs illustrate the story of how two important men, Father Miguel Hidalgo and President Benito Juarez, lead Mexico's fight for independence first from Spain and then from France.

Booktalk

Today, Mexicans and Mexican Americans still celebrate Cinco de Mayo. They dance, play music, and feast on traditional Mexican foods. But do you know why this day is so important to Mexico?

Learning Extensions (Social Studies, Research Skills)

Have children find Mexico on the map and research Mexican history. Who are some of the heroes of Mexican history? The United States has Betsy Ross, George Washington, Abraham Lincoln, and others. See if you can find comparable figures from Mexico.

Schaefer, Lola M. *Cinco de Mayo.* Mankato, Minn.: Capstone Press, 2001. 24p. $14.60. ISBN 0-7368-0661-X.

 📖 PICTURE BOOK—Nonfiction
 Ages 5–8

Summary

Each two-page spread features a full-color photograph and no more than three sentences describing the Mexican celebration of May 5 that commemorates the Mexican victory over the French army in 1862.

Read-Aloud

Full-color photographs and simple text lend themselves to showing the pictures and reading aloud.

Learning Extensions

Develop a K-W-L (what we Know, what do we Want to know, and what have we Learned) chart. To find out what they want to know, have children visit the following Internet sites that are listed in the back of the book: www.worldbook.com/fun/cinco/html/cinco.htm, www.cincodemayo.net/eng/history.htm, and www.mexonline.com/cinco.htm.

Vazquez, Sarah. *Cinco de Mayo.* Austin, Tex.: Raintree Steck-Vaughn, 1999. 31p. $37.00ISBN 0-8172-5562-1.

 📖 PICTURE BOOK—Nonfiction
 Ages 7–12

Summary

Each two-page spread is titled and features photographs, pictures, and short paragraphs, each with a heading. The book begins by describing the fiesta that celebrates the national holiday of Cinco de Mayo and continues with descriptions of the Mexican people and their festivals, costumes, music, dances, parades and parties, and food. A discussion about President Benito Juarez and the Battle of Pueblo are included.

Bookwalk

Turn the pages and talk about the pictures.

Learning Extensions (Research Skills, Art)

Have children research the Native peoples of Mexico—the Olmec, Mayan, and Aztecs—and write reports on one group. Follow up by having each child make a Farolito (lighted bag). Directions are in the back of the book. Serve Polvorones (Mexican cookies). The recipe is in the back of the book.

Other Books to Use for Cinco de Mayo

Flanagan, Alice K. *Cinco de Mayo.* Minneapolis: Compass Point Books, 2004. Ages 4–8. 32p. Illustrated by Patrick Girouard. $22.60. ISBN 0-756-50480-5.

Gnojewski, Carol. *Cinco de Mayo: Celebrating Hispanic Pride.* Berkeley Heights, N.J.: Enslow Publishers, 2002. Ages 7–10. 48p. $23.93. ISBN 0-7660-1525-0.

Wade, Mary Dodson. *Cinco de Mayo.* New York: Childrens Press, 2003. Ages 4–8. 32p. Illustrated by Nancy Reginelli Vargus. $5.95. ISBN 0-516-274899.

6.3 MOTHER'S DAY

Breakfast in bed and family gatherings mark the celebration of Mother's Day on the second Sunday of May. President Woodrow Wilson proclaimed Mother's Day a national holiday in 1914. Yet the observance of a day to honor mothers originated with the ancient Greeks who honored Rhea, whom they believed to be the mother of the their gods. In England during the 1600s, the fourth Sunday of Lent came to be known as Mothering Sunday. This was a day on which servants were given the day off to spend with their mothers. It was Julia Ward Howe who introduced Mother's Day to the United States in 1872. In 1907, Ann Jarvis campaigned for a National Mother's Day to be celebrated on the second Sunday of May. By 1911, Mother's Day was celebrated in every state. Now Mother's

Day is celebrated around the world with Denmark, Finland, Italy, Turkey, Australia, and Belgium observing the holiday on the second Sunday of May.

Baker, Liza. *I Love You Because You're You.* New York: Scholastic, 2001. Unpaged. Illustrated by David McPhail. $9.95. ISBN 0-439-20638-3.

 PICTURE BOOK—Fiction
Ages 3 and up

Summary

Mama Wolf tells Baby Wolf that she loves him when he's happy; when he's sleepy; when he's silly; when he's frightened, bashful, and brave; and when he's many other ways as well.

Read-Aloud

Repetitive, rhythmic language, two lines per page, and simple, cartoonlike illustrations make this book a good read-aloud.

Learning Extensions (Language Arts)

Engage children in a discussion about mother love—about all the ways their mothers, family members, or caregivers love them.

Minchella, Nancy. *Mama Will Be Home Soon.* New York: Scholastic, 2003. Unpaged. Illustrated by Keiko Narahashi. $15.95. ISBN 0-439-38491-5.

 PICTURE BOOK—Fiction
Ages 3–8

Summary

Grandma reassures Lili that Mama will be home soon when Mama goes away for a few days.

Booktalk

Before Mama leaves, she tells Lili that she will see her yellow hat when she returns. Lili is watching for that yellow hat. She sees her yellow sundress hanging on the line. She sees a yellow balloon at the circus. And she sees a bright yellow umbrella at the beach. But when will she see Mama's yellow hat again?

Learning Extensions (Art)

Have children play a color game like I See Something and then draw pictures of Mama's yellow hat.

Strauss, Anna. *Hush, Mama Loves You.* New York: Walker & Co., 2002. Unpaged. Illustrated by Alice Priestley. $15.95. ISBN 0-8027-8806-8.

 📖 PICTURE BOOK—Fiction
 All Ages

Summary

Sara's mother loved and comforted her through falls and hurts, the first day of school, teasing and hurt feelings, failed tests, Sara's teen years, and her first boyfriend. Sara grew up, married, and now has a little girl named Natalie. Sara and Sara's mom love and comfort Natalie just as Sara had been comforted.

Read-Aloud

Read aloud and encourage children to chime in on the recurring refrain that begins with "Close your eyes, my baby."

Learning Extensions (Language Arts, Art)

Share with the children a story about how your mother comforted you when you were a child. Then encourage children to share ways their mothers (or other parents or caregivers) comfort them. They can draw a picture or write about that time—or design a thank-you card for their moms or caregivers.

Weeks, Sarah. *Angel Face.* New York: Atheneum Books for Young Readers, 2002. Unpaged. $17.95. ISBN 0-689-83302-4.

 📖 PICTURE BOOK—Fiction
 Ages 3–7

Summary

When Angel wanders away from his mother, she describes him to the old crow and sends him looking for Angel. This is a book to be seen and heard with its lyrical language and brilliant illustrations.

Read-Aloud

Read the book to the children.

Learning Extensions (Music, Language Arts)

Follow up by playing the CD, a retelling in song and music that is attached to the inside back cover of the book. Then place the book where the children can read and re-read.

Other Books to Use for Mother's Day

Banks, Kate. *Mama's Coming Home.* New York: Frances Foster Books, 2003. Ages 3–6. Unpaged. Illustrated by Tomek Bogacki. $16.00. ISBN 0-374-34747-6.

Lukes, Catherine. *Hooray for Mother's Day.* New York: Simon Spotlight/Nick Jr., 2003. Ages 4–8. Unpaged. Illustrated by Bernie Cavender. $5.99. ISBN 0-689-85241-X.

McCourt, Lisa. *The Most Thankful Thing.* New York: Scholastic, 2004. Ages 4–8. Unpaged. Illustrated by Cyd Moore. $15.95. ISBN 0-439-65083-6.

7
June

INTRODUCTION

Flag Day, Father's Day, and Juneteenth provide opportunities to celebrate patriotism, family relationships, and freedom. Children meet Betsy Ross and Caroline Pickersgill, learn about the history of our flag, and design and make their own flags. Books about Father's Day provide opportunities to reflect on and thank fathers, a family member, or caregiver for their love and comfort. Finally, a book about Juneteenth provides opportunities to learn about the slaves in Texas who were the last to hear of their emancipation in 1865.

7.1 FLAG DAY

In 1916, President Woodrow Wilson proclaimed June 14 National Flag Day. Flag Day is a day to honor our country's flag and its designers and makers by displaying the flag. It was seamstress Betsy Ross who designed and made the first flag at the request of George Washington in 1776. Because the flag represents our independence and unity as a nation, it deserves respect. The following rules govern how it is to be displayed:

1. Fly the flag from sunrise to sunset.
2. Raise the flag briskly and lower it slowly with ceremony.
3. If the flag is flown at night, shine a light on it.
4. Do not fly the flag in rain or inclement weather.
5. Fly the flag at half-staff for 30 days after a tragedy or death.
6. Fly the flag with the stars and blue field at the top.
7. Fly the flag at the top of the pole, with state and other flags below it.
8. Never allow the flag to touch the ground.
9. Burn or bury old flags with ceremony.

Bennett, William J., ed. "Betsy Ross." In *Our Country's Founders: A Book of Advice for Young People* (pp. 31–33). New York: Aladdin Paperbacks, 2001. 314p. $10.00. ISBN 0-689-84469-7.

 📖 CHAPTER BOOK—Nonfiction
   Ages 10 and up

Summary

"Betsy Ross" tells of how Betsy Ross designed and made the first flag with stars and stripes.

Booktalk

Betsy Ross made a lot of things. In fact, she was known for her abilities not only as a seamstress but as a designer as well. Betsy embroidered the ruffles on George Washington's shirts even before he became commander in chief of the military. Then one day, Betsy's uncle, Colonel Ross, a gentleman named Robert Morris, and General Washington asked Betsy to make a flag for the new country. General Washington showed her a sketch of what they thought the flag should look like. Betsy had several suggestions, and she became the designer of the first flag. What did Betsy suggest?

Learning Extensions (Art, Social Studies, Research Skills)

Have children research other flags and their history and origins and then design their own flags.

Greene, Stephanie. *Childhood of Famous Americans: Betsy Ross and the Silver Thimble.* New York: Aladdin Paperbacks, 2002. Unpaged. Illustrated by Diana Magnuson. $3.99. ISBN 0-689-84054-0.

 CHAPTER BOOK—Fiction
 Ages 6–8

Summary

When Betsy Ross was a little girl, she wanted to use her father's tools and help him make a table just like her brother, George. When she cut her finger with the saw, her mother gave Betsy a silver thimble and encouraged her to do what she loved doing: sew.

Booktalk

Have you ever tried to do something just because someone told you that you couldn't do it? Well, Betsy Ross did. When Betsy's brother, George, told her that she couldn't make furniture because she was a girl, Betsy decided to show him that she could! She found some wood in Papa's shop, took the saw from the shelf, and sawed and sawed and sawed. The only thing she cut was her own finger. Mama asked Betsy if she really wanted to make furniture. What do you think Betsy said?

Learning Extensions (Language Arts, Critical Thinking)

Discuss with the children what it is that they really like to do. What do they do well? What would they like to do well? How do they think they can learn how to do it?

Hoose, Phillip. "Caroline Pickersgill: Stitching the Star-Spangled Banner." In *We Were There, Too! Young People in U.S. History* (pp. 79–81). New York: Farrar, Straus & Giroux, 2001. 264p. $26.00. ISBN 0-374-38252-2.

 📖 PICTURE BOOK—Nonfiction
  Ages 10 and up

Summary

This chapter tells of 13-year-old Caroline Pickersgill and her mother, grandmother, and two cousins who stitched the giant flag that flew over Fort McHenry in Baltimore Harbor during the War of 1812, when Francis Scott Key wrote "The Star-Spangled Banner."

Booktalk

Caroline Pickersgill was 13 years old. Her cousins, Eliza and Mary Young, were 13 and 15 when they helped Caroline's mother and grandmother sew the gigantic flag that flew over Fort McHenry in Baltimore Harbor during the War of 1812. The flag was bigger than the Pickersgills' house. Can you imagine a flag bigger than your house? Have you heard of this famous flag? Did you know it still exists today?

Learning Extensions (Music, Language Arts)

Teach the children to sing "The Star-Spangled Banner." Take time to develop the meaning of the words based on the account in this book.

Another Book to Use for Flag Day

Bartoletti, Susan Campbell. *The Flag Maker.* Boston: Houghton Mifflin, 2004. Ages 6–10. 32p. Illustrated by Claire A. Nivola. $16.00. ISBN 0-618-26757-3.

7.2 FATHER'S DAY

The idea of honoring fathers originated in 1909. By 1924, the observance of Father's Day was widespread. In 1966, President Lyndon Johnson signed a presidential proclamation declaring the third Sunday of June National Father's Day.

Bradman, Tony. *Daddy's Lullaby.* New York: Margaret K. McElderry Books, 2001. Unpaged. Illustrated by Jason Cockcroft. $16.95. ISBN 0-689-84295-3.

 📖 PICTURE BOOK—Fiction
  Ages 6 months and up

Summary

Lyrical text and gentle illustrations depict Daddy and baby as they tiptoe through the house, sing a lullaby, and drop off to sleep.

Read-Aloud

Read aloud and show the pictures.

Learning Extensions (Language Arts)

Although the book is written for children six months to two years, children three to seven years will enjoy hearing about how Daddy loved them when they were babies. Ask children to share stories of how their daddies, family members, or caregivers love them. They can create a thank-you card for their dads, family members, or caregivers too.

Browne, Anthony. *My Dad.* New York: Farrar, Straus & Giroux, 2000. Unpaged. $16.00. ISBN 0-374-35101-5.

 📖 PICTURE BOOK—Fiction
  Ages 3–7

Summary

This simple picture book uses hyperbole, metaphor, and simile to sing the praises of "my dad."

Booktalk

Read aloud and show the pictures.

Learning Extensions (Language Arts, Art)

The simple, rhythmic text lends itself to repeated readings. After reading the story aloud to the children, read again and encourage the children to read along with you. Follow up by inviting the children to talk about their dads (or other parent) using the language of the book. For example, "My dad isn't afraid of *anything,* even ..." or "He's as strong as ..." or "He's as happy as ..." Using the book as a model, have the children write one sentence and draw a picture about their dads.

Browne, Michael Dennis. *Give Her the River: A Father's Wish for His Daughter.* New York: Atheneum Books for Young Readers, 2004. Unpaged. Illustrated by Wendell Minor. $15.95. ISBN 0-689-84326-7.

 PICTURE BOOK—Fiction
 Ages 4–8

Summary

A father expresses his love for his daughter by sharing with her the life of a river—the water, the sky, the shore, and the wildlife.

Bookwalk

Come! Let's join a girl and her father as the father expresses his love for her by sharing with her the life of a river. Turn the pages and show each two-page spread as you talk about the illustrations. For example, begin by saying, "Swans glide by in the early morning. Then the girl plays in the water under the willows. She sees the swallows fly overhead—the blue wildflowers growing here—and shiny leaves. Soon the geese swim by. The girl and her father lay in a hammock to read—and sit on a bench—while a Scottie passes by. See the cloud in the sky—then the stars—and here is a heron. The girl can drift in a canoe—sail with her friends—or watch the ducklings." Show the endpapers and say, "The river is her special place." Ask, "Do you have a special place?"

Learning Extensions (Language Arts)

Ask children if they have special places that they share with someone they love. Encourage discussion of their special places and special people.

McCormick, Wendy, and Jennifer Eachus. *Daddy, Will You Miss Me?* New York: Aladdin Paperbacks, 2002. Unpaged. $6.99. ISBN 0-689-85063-8.

 📖 PICTURE BOOK—Fiction
 Ages 2–8

Summary

A boy and his daddy feel badly because they will be separated for four weeks when Daddy goes to Africa. Daddy comforts the boy by telling him that he will whisper his name and blow him kisses. The boy says that he will mark off each day on the calendar and save daily treasures to show Daddy when he returns.

Booktalk

Africa is a long way away. This little boy's daddy is going to Africa for four weeks. The boy and his daddy are sad. But Daddy says that he will whisper the boy's name to the wind and blow kisses over the sky. He says (read aloud the second paragraph on the third two-page spread and the first paragraph on the fourth two-page spread.) After Daddy said that, the boy knew what he could do for Daddy.

Learning Extensions (Language Arts)

Ask children if they have ever been separated from someone they love. Ask them to share how they found comfort and maintained close ties during the separation.

Other Books to Use for Father's Day

Banks, Steven. *Pick a Dad, Any Dad!* New York: Simon Spotlight/Nick Jr., Ages 4–8. 24p. Illustrated by Harry Moore. $5.50. ISBN 0-689-97185-6.

Ernest, Lisa Campbell. *That Is the Van That Dad Cleaned.* New York: Simon & Schuster Books for Young Readers, 2005. Ages 3–7. 40p. $15.95. ISBN 0-689-86190-7.

Loomis, Christine. *The 10 Best Things About My Dad.* New York: Cartwheel Books, 2004. Ages 4–8. 32p. Illustrated by Jackie Urbanovic. $3.50. ISBN 0-439-57769-1.

7.3 JUNETEENTH

On January 1, 1980, Juneteenth, that is, June 19, became an official state holiday in Texas. Juneteenth is the oldest known celebration of the ending of slavery. It was not until 1865, two and a half years after Lincoln's Emancipation Proclamation on January 1, 1863, that Union soldiers brought the news to Galveston, Texas, that the Civil War had ended and that the slaves were free. The day is celebrated with rodeos, fishing, barbecues, baseball games, guest speakers, and prayer services.

Branch, Muriel Miller. *Juneteenth: Freedom Day.* New York: Cobblehill, 1998. 54p. Photographs by Willis Branch. $15.99. ISBN 0-525-65222-1.

 CHAPTER BOOK—Nonfiction; African-American
 Ages 10–14

Summary

The author and her husband travel to Texas to celebrate Juneteenth. She explains the history of the holiday and how its observance spread from Texas across the country. She then describes the many ways in which it is celebrated today.

Booktalk

Free at last! Juneteenth is a freedom celebration that began on June 19, 1865, in Galveston, Texas, when the slaves learned the news of their emancipation. The Emancipation Proclamation became effective on January 1, 1863. The Civil War ended in April 1865. Why didn't the slaves in Texas hear the news of their freedom until June 19, 1865? And where does the name "Juneteenth" come from?

Learning Extensions (Language Arts, Music)

Plan a reenactment of the story. Begin with a reading of the Emancipation Proclamation. Encourage students to express how the slaves must have felt when they heard the news of their freedom. Then have students plan a celebration by using the suggestions on page 49 and by writing to the national organizations whose addresses are on page 50. Be sure to include music such as "In the Great Getting Up Morning," "Free at Last," "The Star-Spangled Banner," and "America the Beautiful."

An extensive bibliography at the end of the book lists books, periodicals, and newspapers that tell more about Juneteenth.

Other Books to Use for Juneteenth

McKissack, Patricia, and Frederick McKissack. *Days of Jubilee.* New York: Scholastic, 2003. Ages 10 and up. 134p. $15.95. ISBN 0-590-10764-X.

Weatherford, Carole Boston. *Juneteenth Jamboree.* Boston: Lee & Low, 1995. Ages 4–8. Unpaged. Illustrated by Yvonne Buchanan. $19.90. ISBN 1-880000-18-0.

8
July

INTRODUCTION

Three July holidays, Canada Day, Independence Day, and Pioneer Day, celebrate independence and freedom. Canada and the United States celebrate independence from England on July 1 and July 4, respectively. Mormons celebrate their freedom to live and worship in the new homeland founded by Brigham Young and his followers at the site of what now is Salt Lake City, Utah. Children learn the history of Canada's independence; meet our founding fathers, such as George Washington and others; explore life in America during the seventeenth century; clean up Independence Hall and wait on delegates to the Constitutional Convention with Charlie Brown and friends; and travel by wagon train with Mary Goble and her family to Salt Lake City. Learning Extensions include map activities, songs, Readers Theater, creating a class book, and other language arts and social studies activities.

8.1 CANADA DAY

Canada Day, July 1, celebrates Canada's independence from England as a self-governing, unified country. That independence and unification began with the formation of the Dominion of Canada on July 1, 1867. Canada expanded to take in British Columbia and Victoria, Prince Edward Island, and Arctic territories until 1880. During that time, boundaries with the United States and Alaska were defined. Finally, in 1949, Newfoundland entered the Dominion of Canada.

Murphy, Patricia J. *Canada Day.* New York: Childrens Press, 2002. 31p. $19.50. ISBN 0-516-22662-2.

    EASY READER—Nonfiction
    Ages 5–8

Summary

Color photographs and simple text explain the history of Canada's independence and describe the celebration of Canada's Independence Day.

Booktalk

Canada is our neighbor to the north. (Show children where Canada is on a world map.) In the United States, we celebrate our independence from England on July 4. Canada celebrates its independence from England on July 1. But Canada did not have to fight a war with England. How do you suppose Canada became an independent country?

Learning Extensions (Social Studies, Music)

On a map of the world, have the children find Canada. Ask a child to trace with a pointer the outline of the 10 provinces and three territories. Honor Canada's celebration of its independence by teaching the children to sing the Canadian national anthem, "O Canada!"

Other Book to Use for Canada Day

Harrison, Ted. *O Canada.* New York: Tichnor & Fields, 1993. All ages. Unpaged. $19.00. ISBN 0-3395-660750.

8.2 INDEPENDENCE DAY

Independence Day falls on July 4 and is the greatest secular holiday in the United States. July 4 marks the anniversary of the Declaration of Independence issued in 1776 by the Continental Congress. The Declaration of Independence declared the 13 colonies independent from England. The holiday is celebrated with parades, fireworks, patriotic speeches, military displays, games, athletic contests, and picnics.

Bennett, William J., ed. *Our Country's Founders: A Book of Advice for Young People.* New York: Aladdin Paperbacks, 2001. 314p. $10.00. ISBN 0-689-84469-7.

 CHAPTER BOOK—Nonfiction
 Ages 10 and up

Summary

This is a collection of writings from our founding fathers—George Washington, Thomas Jefferson, John Adams, Benjamin Rush, Benjamin Franklin, Patrick Henry, and others. Their writings are organized according to seven topics: patriotism and courage, love and courtship, civility and friendship, education of the head and heart, industry and frugality, justice, and piety. The Declaration of Independence, the Constitution of the United States, and the Bill of Rights are included. The book ends with brief biographies of each contributor, a time line of the American Revolution, and additional sources.

Booktalk

George Washington, Thomas Jefferson, Benjamin Franklin—you know these names. They are the founders of our country. But what did they actually say and think? What did George Washington write to his adopted grandson and to his nephews? What did Thomas Jefferson put in his letters to his daughters? Read the advice that Benjamin Franklin and Noah Webster gave to young people, and read letters between friends such as Thomas Jefferson and James Madison. Excerpts from George Washington's inaugural address, Thomas Jefferson's draft of the Declaration of Independence, and the final copy of the Declaration of Independence are some of the other interesting things you'll find in this book. Explore the minds of these great leaders.

Learning Extensions (Language Arts)

Select excerpts appropriate to your children's interests or your course of study to read aloud or retell. Revisit the text by having children select excerpts of their choice and creating Readers Theater scripts from the excerpts. Plan a performance in which you and your children will introduce our country's founders to other groups of children, families, or friends by hosting a Readers Theater production.

Borden, Louise. *America Is ...* New York: Margaret K. McElderry Books, 2002. Unpaged. Illustrated by Stacey Schuett. $16.95. ISBN 0-6-89-83900-6.

 📖 PICTURE BOOK—Nonfiction
 Ages 6–9

Summary

Poetic text and bright, colorful illustrations pay tribute to America—to the nation and its states; its flag, pledge of allegiance, and national anthem; its land of farms and cities, lakes and rivers, prairies, deserts, and mountains; and its many peoples.

Read-Aloud

Read aloud the poetic text and show the illustrations as you turn each page.

Learning Extensions (Language Arts, Art)

Using the book as a model, have your children create a class book about your community. Generate a group list, naming the attributes of your community—your school, your town, or your state. Have each child select an attribute, then create and illustrate a page. Title your book *The Name of Our Community Is ...*

Masoff, Joy. *Chronicle of America: American Revolution: 1700–1800.* New York: Scholastic, 2000. 48p. Illustrated with photographs from America's Living History Museums. $15.95. ISBN 0-439-05109-6.

   📖 PICTURE BOOK—Nonfiction
   Ages 9–14

Summary

A one-page introduction and one-page conclusion with 21 two-page spreads give an account of life during the seventeenth century, the time of the American Revolution. Color photos and drawings, recipes, games, and vignettes supplement the text.

Booktalk

If you were living during the American Revolution, what would your life be like? How would you dress? What would you eat? What would you do for fun? Find out what "pop goes the weasel" means and why Yankee Doodle stuck a feather in his cap and called it "macaroni." All this and more can be found in *Chronicle of America: American Revolution: 1700–1800.* (Show book.)

Learning Extensions (Social Studies, Research Skills)

Use the books and Web sites listed at the back of the book and identified in the following to research more information about the era. Use the book as a model to organize and report additional information. Use the recipe on page 12 to make and serve Apple Tansy. Encourage the children to play colonial games, such as backgammon and checkers or marble, dice, and card games.

Schultz, Charles M. *Peanuts: Here's to You America!* New York: Little Simon, 2002. Unpaged. $5.99. ISBN 0-689-85163-4.

   📖 PICTURE BOOK—Fiction
   Ages 7–12

Summary

Charlie Brown and friends clean up Independence Hall, then wait on the colonial delegates to the Constitutional Convention in Philadelphia in 1787.

Booktalk

Lucy says we should have a beautiful queen instead of a president. But Lucy's job at the Constitutional Convention in Philadelphia in

1787 is not to make decisions. Her job is to mop the floor while Marcie and Peppermint Patty haul water to the delegates. All summer long, the delegates argue about the form of government they are creating. Linus, Charlie Brown—they're all here, and they'll show you how our government was formed. Read *Here's to You, America!* (Show book.)

Learning Extensions (Social Studies)

Use this book as a springboard to a study of the three branches (legislative, judicial, and executive) of our government. Have children make a chart of the government showing the powers of each. Then ask them to explain what is meant by "balance of power" between the three branches of government.

Other Books to Use for Independence Day

Bobrick, Benson. *Fight for Freedom: The American Revolutionary War.* New York: Atheneum Books for Young Readers, 2004. All ages. 96p. $22.95. ISBN 0-689-86422-1.

Borden, Louise. *Sleds on Boston Common: A Story from the American Revolution.* New York: Margaret K. McElderry Books, 2000. Ages 9–12. Unpaged. Illustrated by Robert Andrew Parker. $17.00. ISBN 0-689-82812-8.

Gregory, Kristiana. *We Are Patriots: Hope's Revolutionary War Diary.* New York: Scholastic, 2002. Ages 7–9. 112p. $10.95. ISBN 0-439-221039-9.

8.3 PIONEER DAY (MORMON)

Pioneer Day is observed on July 24 and is also called Covered Wagon Days and Days of '47. Pioneer Day is a Utah state holiday and is the greatest Mormon holiday. It celebrates the arrival of Brigham Young and his followers, the Church of Jesus Christ of Latter Day Saints, at the site of Salt Lake City on July 24, 1847. The holiday is celebrated with parades, devotionals, sporting events, feasts, dances, excursions, and reunions.

Hoose, Phillip. "Mary Goble: Walking to Zion." In *We Were There, Too! Young People in U.S. History* (pp.138–42). New York: Farrar, Straus & Giroux, 2001. 264p. $26.00. ISBN 0-374-388252-2.

📖 PICTURE BOOK—Nonfiction
Ages 10 and up

Summary

After Mary Goble and her family joined the Mormon Church in Sussex, England, they sailed from Liverpool to Boston; traveled by train to Iowa City, where they bought a wagon and a team of oxen; and joined a wagon train to Salt Lake City, Utah, that they called Zion.

Booktalk

By the time they reach Zion, Mary and two other members of her family are suffering from severe frostbite. But they are the lucky ones. Mary's two sisters and mother have died along the way. It is a long and hard journey from Sussex, England, to Salt Lake City, Utah, traveling by ship, train, and wagon train. This is a true story about a real pioneer who helped settle the West.

Learning Extensions (Social Studies)

On a map, trace Mary's journey from Sussex, England, to Liverpool; across the ocean by way of Newfoundland to Boston; by train to Iowa City; and finally by wagon through Iowa and Nebraska to Utah.

Other Books to Use for Pioneer Day

Gunderson, Mary. *Oregon Trail Cooking.* Mankato, Minn.: Blue Earth Books, 2000. Ages 8–10. 32p. $19.21. ISBN 0-736-80355-6.

King, David C. *Pioneer Days: Discover the Past with Fun Projects, Games, Activities, and Recipes.* New York: John Wiley & Sons,1997. Ages 8–10. 32p. $19.21. ISBN 0-736-803356.

9
August

INTRODUCTION

August is "back-to-school month." Some children are starting school for the first time. Some are changing schools and must make new friends and get to know new teachers. Others are returning to familiar schools, teachers, and friends. Tests, teachers, homework, and new experiences lie ahead. Laugh with the children in Miss Malarky's class as they prepare for The Test, spend a year with Miss Agnes in her school on the Koyukuk River in Alaska, and help Mama Rex and T complete a homework project. Respond to the books by making dioramas, completing sentence starters, and doing other language arts activities.

9.1 BACK TO SCHOOL

The New England colonies, particularly Massachusetts, were the birthplace of public schooling in the United States. Initially, religion played a major role in colonial schools. As it became increasingly difficult to accommodate diverse religious groups, schooling focused on the development of reading and writing and meeting the practical needs of the community. With the establishment of a new republic based on the ideals of democracy, equality, and freedom came the development of a system of common schools that were free, universal, and open to all. By the middle of the nineteenth century, religious instruction had disappeared from the school curriculum. A free system of public education that was publicly controlled and supported was in place. With that, the United States became the first country to provide universal education marked by separation of church and state.

Finchler, Judy. *Testing Miss Malarkey.* New York: Walker & Co., 2000. Unpaged. Illustrated by Kevin O'Malley. $15.95. ISBN 0-8027-8737-1.

  PICTURE BOOK—Fiction
  Ages 5–9

Summary

Humor prevails as everyone prepares for The Test (Instructional Performance Through Understanding test): teachers, students, the principal, the cafeteria lady, the school janitor, parents—even the PTA.

Booktalk

At school, everyone is getting ready for The Test. We kids are playing Multiplication Mambo and Funny Phonics. Miss Malarky bites her nails. The principal screams for pencils. Even the PTA gets involved in the excitement. What happens when your school prepares for The Test?

Learning Extensions (Language Arts)

Use the book as a model for humorous writing. Have children add humorous endings to sentence starters such as "My teacher …" "At recess ..." "Our principal ..." "The cafeteria lady ..." or "During gym ..."

Hill, Kirkpatrick. *The Year of Miss Agnes*. New York: Margaret K. McElderry Books, 2000. 115p. $16.00. ISBN 0-689-82933-7.

 📖 CHAPTER BOOK—Fiction; Native American; Alaska
  Ages 8–12

Summary

Miss Agnes is the teacher from England who touches and changes the lives of the Athabascan villagers who live on the Koyukuk River in Alaska.

Booktalk

Miss Agnes is strong. She wears pants! Miss Agnes is a teacher who came all the way to Alaska from another country—England. Miss Agnes is the best. Do you want to know why? Do you want to find out what it's like to grow up in a small Alaskan village on the Koyukuk River? I'll tell you—in *A Year with Miss Agnes*.

Learning Extensions (Language Arts)

Read the book aloud with your group and trace the development of each of the characters. How do Fred, her sister Bokka, her Mamma, and her classmates grow and change during their year with Miss Agnes? Make a chart of the characters and list the changes.

Rogers, Jacqueline. *Kindergarten ABC*. New York: Scholastic, 2002. Unpaged. $10.95. ISBN 0-439-36837-5.

 📖 PICTURE BOOK—ABC Book
  Ages 4–7

Summary

An activity is named for each letter of the alphabet. Each letter is given a day. For example, on "Bb" day, we bring backpacks. A search-and-find game is included on each page. For example, look for a ball, books, or a braid.

Read-Aloud

Read aloud and show the pictures. Invite children to predict what the activity might be. Stimulate interest in this book by inviting children to search for listed items in the pictures.

Learning Extensions (Language Arts)

Have children identify and list additional items they can find for each letter of the alphabet.

Vail, Rachel. *Mama Rex & T: Homework Trouble.* New York: Orchard Books, 2001. Unpaged. Illustrated by Steve Bjorkman. $14.95. ISBN 0-4-39-40628-5.

 📖 BEGINNING CHAPTER BOOK—Fiction
   Ages 6–9

Summary

When Mama Rex got off work early, she planned to spend the afternoon with T and surprised T by picking him at school. T surprised Mama Rex with a homework project due tomorrow. Together they visited the library, the Museum of Natural History, and the park. At home, T put together his diorama with a lot of help from Mama Rex.

Book Talk

Oops! T forgot to tell Mama Rex that he has to make a diorama— and it's due tomorrow. What does a dinosaur make a diorama about? Well, pigs, of course, but all T knows about pigs is that one went to market and another stayed home. And what is a diorama anyway?

Learning Extensions (Art)

Use this book to introduce dioramas to the children. Make dioramas about animals like T and his classmates made. As the children read the book, discuss what a diorama is, where you can find information about animals, what materials you can use, and how to make a diorama. Like Mama Rex, you may even want to take the children to the library, a natural history museum, and the park.

Other Books to Use for School

Catalanotto, Peter. *Matthew A.B.C.* New York: A Richard Jackson Books, 2001. Ages 4–6. Unpaged. $14.95. ISBN 0-689-84582-0.

MacDonald, Amy. *No More Nasty.* New York: Melanie Kroupa Books, 2001. Ages 8–12. Illustrated by Cat Bowman Smith. $16.00. ISBN 0-374-35529-0.

Wood, Douglas. *What Teachers Can't Do.* New York: Simon & Schuster Books for Young Readers, 2002. Ages 3–8. Unpaged. Illustrated by Doug Cushman. $14.95. ISBN 0-689-84644-4.

10

September

INTRODUCTION

September is National Hispanic Heritage Month, a time to honor the contributions of Spanish-speaking Americans to our county's history and culture. Meet a little girl who visits Grandma and Grandpa, her father's parents, on Saturdays, and Abuelito y Abuelita, her mother's parents, on Sundays; then meet don Ignacio's faithful servant Juan Verdades, and finally visit Artura in the Los Angeles barrio where he lives and Eric, who spends his summers with his grandmother in Spanish Harlem.

September is also the month we celebrate Labor Day, Grandparents' Day, and Rosh Hashanah. Children will read about workers and their jobs, Lulu's Greek grandmother who embarrasses her by singing in unexpected places,

Gershon's monster, and others. Learning Extensions include Readers Theater, creating a collage, and researching labor conditions, early strikes, efforts to unionize in the late 1800s and early 1900s and other activities related to language arts, social studies, art, music, values education, character education, and critical thinking.

10.1 NATIONAL HISPANIC HERITAGE MONTH

National Hispanic Heritage Month begins on September 15 and ends on October 15. Hispanic refers to Spanish-speaking people of any race in the United States. The Spanish were the earliest settlers in the New World. On September 15, five countries (Costa Rica, El Salvador, Guatemala, Honduras, and Nicaragua) gained their independence. In 1968, National Hispanic Heritage Week was proclaimed for the week of September 15. In 1988, the observance was extended to a full month. The purpose of the month is to honor the contributions of Hispanics to America's history and culture.

Ada, Alma Flor. *I Love Saturdays y Domingos.* New York: Atheneum Books for Young Readers, 2002. Unpaged. Illustrated by Elivia Savadier. $16.95. ISBN 0-689-31819-7.

 PICTURE BOOK—Fiction; Bilingual
Ages 5–8

Summary

On the weekend, a child visits her grandparents. On Saturdays, she visits Grandma and Grandpa, her father's parents. On Sundays, she visits Abuelito y Abuelita, her mother's parents. This is a bilingual book written mainly in English. When the child visits her Mexican-American grandparents, Spanish is used.

Booktalk

When I visit Grandma and Grandpa, I listen to their stories, play with Grandma's cat, watch the fish in Grandpa's aquarium, and run with a bunch of balloons. When I visit Abuelito y Abuelita, I listen to their stories, play with Abuelita's dog, go to the circus, and fly a kite. When my birthday comes, they all come to my house and make my birthday special. What do you do when you visit your grandparents? Do they make your birthday special?

Learning Extensions (Language Arts)

Encourage children to talk about their families and cultural traditions. If you have children from bicultural/bilingual families, ask them to share with the group how they celebrate and honor their bicultural heritage. Invite children to share their experiences with their grandparents. What are their grandparents like? Finally, ask them to tell the group how their grandparents make their birthdays special.

Hayes, Joe. *Juan Verdades: The Man Who Couldn't Tell a Lie.* New York: Orchard Books, 2001. Unpaged. Illustrated by Joseph Daniel Fiedler. $16.95. ISBN 0-439-293311-1.

 PICTURE BOOK—Fiction
 Ages 8–12

Summary

Juan Verdades is the faithful servant who saves face by telling a riddle rather than a lie. A note to readers and storytellers at the back of the book explains the origins and variations of this story of "The Faithful Servant."

Booktalk

Don Ignacio is so sure of his servant's faithfulness and honesty that he gambles his ranch against don Arturo's ranch. Will don Arturo be able to trick Juan Verdades into telling a lie? But wait, don Arturo's daughter Araceli has a plan so that both men can win the bet. One man loses his ranch, but neither man loses his ranch. How can that be?

Learning Extension (Language Arts, Values Education)

Engage children in a discussion of honesty, right and wrong, and the meaning of being trustworthy. Ask them to think about and describe people in their lives who are honest and trustworthy. Then ask them to think about and give an example of themselves being honest and trustworthy.

Johnston, Tony. *Any Small Goodness: A Novel of the Barrio.* New York: Blue Sky Press, 2001. 128p. Illustrated by Raul Colon. $15.95. ISBN 0-439-18936-5.

 CHAPTER BOOK—Fiction
 Ages 9 and up

Summary

The hard life that Arturo and his family know living in the Los Angeles barrio is tempered by the small kindnesses they experience with each other and their neighbors.

Booktalk

Life in the barrio is hard. Arturo, his family, and their neighbors and friends struggle. But little things make a difference for the good, like the neighbor who sits up all night in the tree with Rosa's lost cat, the NBA basketball player who serves as assistant coach at Arturo's school, and the police officer who replaces Rosa's stolen lunch box. Papa tells Arturo that you must create good if you do not find it. And Arturo does. Find out how.

Learning Extensions (Language Arts, Values Education)

Discuss the term "barrio." Engage children in a discussion of the small kindnesses they experience in their daily lives. Ask them to think about how they can share small kindnesses with each other. Then ask each child to write a contract with himself or herself that says, "I will share small kindnesses by" (name the kindnesses and the people they are for).

Velasquez, Eric. *Grandma's Records.* New York: Walker & Co., 2001. Unpaged. $16.95. ISBN 0-8027-8760-6.

 PICTURE BOOK—Fiction; Spanish Harlem
 Ages 5–8

Summary

Eric spends his summers with his grandmother in Spanish Harlem. Grandma loves the music of her native Puerto Rico and lets Eric select and play her records.

Booktalk

(Introduce this book by playing Grandma's music on the CD that accompanies the book.) This is the music from Puerto Rico that Grandma loves and that Eric listens to. Grandma's nephew, Sammy, plays percussion in the best band in Puerto Rico. When Sammy's band comes to New York for a concert, Sammy gives Grandma two tickets to the concert. At the concert, Eric learns why Grandma's favorite song is so special. Why do you suppose it is?

Learning Extensions (Music)

Ask the children if their family members have favorite music and special songs. Encourage discussion, then invite children to bring CDs or tapes of that favorite music to share with the group.

Another Book to Use for National Hispanic Heritage Month

Johnston, Tony. *The Ancestors Are Singing.* New York: Farrar, Straus & Giroux, 2003. Ages 8 and up. 64p. Illustrated by Karen Barbour. $16.00. ISBN 0-374-30347-9.

10.2 LABOR DAY

The observance of Labor Day originated in Europe in the 1800s and falls on May 1 in most industrialized countries. In Canada and the United States, Labor Day is observed on the first Monday in September. Labor Day became a national holiday in the United States in 1894. Businesses close, and the day is celebrated with picnics, parades, and athletic events.

Banks, Kate. *The Night Worker.* New York: Farrar, Straus & Giroux, 2000. Unpaged. Illustrated by Georg Hallensleben. $16.00. ISBN 0-374-35520-7.

    PICTURE BOOK—Fiction
    Ages 3–7

Summary

Papa is an engineer who works at night. One night, Papa gives a hard hat to Alex and takes Alex to work with him.

Booktalk

What does your daddy do? Alex's daddy is an engineer. He works at night. Do you know what an engineer does? One night Alex goes to work with his daddy. Who else might he see? At the construction site where his daddy works, Alex hears the rattle of heavy equipment, and sees a bulldozer, an excavator, and a cement mixer. He sees a street cleaner, a deliveryman, and a policewoman. What would you see if you went to work with your daddy?

Learning Extensions (Career Education)

Engage the children in a discussion of the kinds of jobs their parents have. What might they see if they went to work with their parents or caregivers? On whiteboard or chart paper, list the jobs and what the children would see. Have the children write a sentence and draw a picture.

Bartoletti, Susan Campbell. *Kids On Strike!* Boston: Houghton Mifflin, 1999. 208p. $8.95. ISBN 0-618-36923-6.

 CHAPTER BOOK—Nonfiction
Ages 10–14

Summary

Eight chapters document the beginnings of the labor movement during the late nineteenth and early twentieth centuries. Accounts of child workers, early strikes, and their leaders agitating for improved working conditions retell the story of the working poor.

Booktalk

Ten-year-old Harriet Hanson is a bobbin girl in Lowell, Massachusetts. Eight-year-old Philip Marcus is a newsboy on the streets of Chicago. Pauline Newman is 16 years old when she loses her job in a New York City garment factory. They and other children and young people have no hope of schooling. How will they better their lives?

Learning Extensions (Social Studies, Language Arts)

Divide children into eight groups. Assign each group a chapter to read. Then have each group report to the whole group about the child workers and their efforts to improve their working conditions.

Burleigh, Robert. *Messenger, Messenger.* New York: Atheneum Books for Young Readers, 2000. Unpaged. Illustrated by Barry Root. $16.00. ISBN 0-689-82103-4.

September

    📖 PICTURE BOOK—Fiction
    Ages 5–7

Summary

Deep, rich, full-page illustrations provide the background for simple repetitive text written in verse that tells about the work of a bicycle messenger in an urban setting.

Read-Aloud

Read aloud.

Learning Extensions (Language Arts, Critical Thinking Skills)

After reading aloud, revisit the text. Develop thinking skills and oral language skills by talking about the pictures. For example, in the first two pages, the messenger is getting up for another day's work. Ask, "What does the picture tell us about the messenger? He has books by his bed and piled on the stove. He probably likes to read but doesn't do much cooking. He has a drum in the corner, a plant and turntable on the windowsill, a stereo speaker in the corner, and a kitten by the feeding bowl. It looks as if the messenger likes music and the kitten is probably hungry." Use the details in the illustrations throughout the book to provide opportunities for language development. Follow the oral discussion with a second oral reading. Encourage the children to chime in on the repetitive language.

Durbin, William. *The Journal of Otto Peltonen, a Finnish Immigrant: Hibbing, Minnesota, 1905.* New York: Scholastic, 2000. 176p. $10.95. ISBN 0-439-09254-X.

    📖 CHAPTER BOOK—Fiction
    Ages 8–14

Summary

Otto and his family migrate from Finland to Hibbing, Minnesota, to work in the iron ore mines. Like other miners, Otto and his family experience the corrupt management, poor wages, and unsafe working conditions that moved miners to form unions, protest working conditions, and stage strikes. Those who did were "blacklisted," fired, and left without employment or company-owned housing. The historical note at the back of the book includes black-and-white photographs that document conditions on "the range" in the early 1900s.

Booktalk

Otto and his family come all the way from Finland to Hibbing, Minnesota, to work in the iron ore mines and at the lumber mill. They live in a tarpaper shack, in weather that sometimes gets as cold as 36 degrees below zero. Why? They want to buy a farm. When Otto turns 16, he works in the mines too. But hard work isn't the only challenge for Otto. The foreman wants a bribe, and the Socialists want him to help organize a union. Otto struggles to decide.

Learning Extensions (Social Studies)

After reading this book, encourage children to research labor conditions, early strikes, and efforts to unionize during the late 1800s and early 1900s.

Other Books to Use for Labor Day

Desimini, Lisa. *Policeman Lou.* New York: Blue Sky Press, 2003. Ages 4–8. Unpaged. $15.95. ISBN 0-439-40888-1.

Ganci, Chris. *Chief: The Life of Peter J. Ganci, a New York City Firefighter.* New York: Orchard Books, 2003. Ages 8 and up. Unpaged. $16.96. ISBN 0-439-44386-5.

Weatherby, Brenda. *The Trucker.* New York: Scholastic, 2004. Ages 4–8. Unpaged. Illustrated by Mark Weatherby. $15.95. ISBN 0-439-39877-0.

10.3 GRANDPARENTS' DAY

In 1978, President Jimmy Carter declared the first Sunday after Labor Day National Grandparents' Day. The idea for a day honoring grandparents originated with Marion McQuade of Fayette County, West Virginia. She was concerned about the lonely and neglected elderly nursing home residents. Governor Arch Moore of West Virginia proclaimed the first Grandparents' Day in 1973. The month of September was chosen for the observance because September signifies the autumn of life. The purpose of the day is to recognize and honor grandparents, to encourage grandparents to show love to their children's children, and to foster awareness of the guidance that older people can offer.

Crunk, Tony. *Grandpa's Overalls.* New York: Orchard Books, 2001. Unpaged. Illustrated by Scott Nash. $15.95. ISBN 0-531-30321-7.

    PICTURE BOOK—Fiction
    Ages 5–8

Summary

When Grandpa's overalls run away, the neighbors lend a hand and do all his work for the day because "a man can't work in nothing but his long-handled drawers."

Booktalk

There they go! Grandpa's overalls! They hopped off their nail on the wall and ran out the door, across the porch, through the yard, over the fence, past the chicken house, and around the barn. We chased those overalls all around—across the garden, the potato patch, the hay, the cornfield, and the orchard. Then all of a sudden, the overalls leaped over the treetops and disappeared into the clouds. Grandpa's never missed a day of work in his life. What will he do without his overalls? We all know that "a man can't work in nothing but his long-handled drawers."

Learning Extensions (Language Arts)

After the Booktalk, encourage children to make predictions about what will happen next. Either read aloud or have the children read to confirm their predictions. Have children retell the story by correctly sequencing events and using the repetitive language that occurs in the book.

D'Arc, Karen Scourby. *My Grandmother Is a Singing Yaya.* New York: Orchard Books, 2001. Unpaged. Illustrated by Diane Palmisciano. $15.95. ISBN 0-439-29309-X.

📖 PICTURE BOOK—Fiction; Greek
Ages 5–8

Summary

Lulu's Greek grandmother ("yaya" is Greek for "grandmother") loves to sing and breaks out in song in unexpected places. Lulu invites her grandmother to the school picnic on Grandparents' Day but fears that she will sing. And she does—at the invitation of the principal.

Booktalk

"Yaya" means "grandmother" in Greek, and Lulu's yaya loves to sing. Sometimes Lulu sings with her. But other times, Lulu feels embarrassed when Yaya sings—like when she sings at the movies or about the dog in the pet store. On Grandparents' Day, Lulu invites Yaya to the school picnic. Lulu hopes Yaya will act like all the other grandparents. She wonders how she can keep Yaya from singing. Lulu knows that she will hurt Yaya's feelings if she asks her not to sing. What can she do?

Learning Extensions (Language Arts)

Ask children if they ever felt embarrassed by a family member or a friend. Do you ever want your family members and friends to act like everyone else? What do you do? Tell children about an embarrassing situation you once had with a family member or friend. Ask the children to share an embarrassing experience with family members or friends.

Mills, Claudia. *Gus and Grandpa at Basketball.* New York: Farrar, Straus & Giroux, 2001. 48p. Illustrated by Catherine Stock. $14.00. ISBN 0-374-32818-8.

📖 BEGINNING CHAPTER BOOK—Fiction
Ages 6–8

Summary

Gus's team loses all its games until Grandpa shares a secret with Gus.

Booktalk

Gus likes to practice basketball. He likes being on the team. But he doesn't really like the games. They're noisy with everybody watching and yelling. Other kids get in his way so that he can't make baskets. Everything happens so fast that Gus gets confused. And Gus's team always loses the game. Then at the very last game, Grandpa teaches Gus a secret. What do you suppose that secret is?

Learning Extensions (Language Arts)

Engage children in a discussion about team sports. What sports do they play? Do they practice? How does playing a game differ from practicing? Did they learn anything like Gus did to help them win the game?

Roth, Susan L. *Grandpa Blows His Penny Whistle Until the Angels Sing.* New York: Barefoot Books, 2001. Unpaged. $16.99. ISBN 1-84148-247-1.

📖 PICTURE BOOK—Fiction
Ages 5–10

Summary

Instead of getting ready for church, Little Boy James runs off on Sunday morning, falls off the barn roof, and doesn't regain consciousness until Grandpa plays his penny whistle and the angels sing. Collage illustrations rich in color and texture supplement the touching text.

Booktalk/Bookwalk

(Show the book as you give the Booktalk.) Instead of putting on his shoes to go to church on a hot Sunday morning, Little Boy James runs out the door, rides Old Thunder, walks the fence, and scrambles into the hayloft and then up a ladder onto the barn roof. Papa tells him to come down. Then Grandpa tells him to come down. All of a sudden, Little Boy flips the ladder, tumbles off the roof, and lands on the ground. He's not dead, just knocked out, but he's not regaining consciousness. Can anything make Little Boy James wake up?

Learning Extensions (Character Education, Language Arts, Art)

Church schools, religious education programs, and families who homeschool their children may have a particular interest in this story of unconditional love and forgiveness of a naughty little boy. Ask children if they were ever like Little Boy James. Did they ever run off, disobey, or do things they were not supposed to do? What happened? Did they get into trouble? Were they punished? Did their families forgive them and continue to love them? Follow up by having children create a collage depicting their own experiences. Use the illustrations in the book as a model for the children's collages. Provide an assortment of textured papers and fabrics for them to use.

Other Books to Use for Grandparents' Day

Best, Cari. *When Catherine the Great and I Were Eight.* New York: Farrar, Straus & Giroux, 2003. Ages 4–8. Unpaged. Illustrated by Giselle Potter. $16.00. ISBN 0-374-39954-9.

Root, Phyllis. *The Name Quilt.* New York: Farrar, Straus & Giroux, 2003. Ages 6–10. Unpaged. Illustrated by Margot Apple. $16.00. ISBN 0-374-35484-7.

Schotter, Roni. *In the Piney Woods.* New York: Melanie Kroupa Books, 2003. Ages 6–10. Unpaged. Illustrated by Kimberly Bulcken Root. $16.00. ISBN 0-374-33623-7.

10.4 ROSH HASHANAH

Rosh Hashanah is the first day of the Jewish New Year and falls on the first day of the Jewish month of Tishri. Rosh Hashanah is the first of the Jewish High Holy Days, the 10 days of repentance that end with Yom Kippur. The blowing of the ram's horn, called the shofar, on Rosh Hashanah is a call to spiritual awakening. The blowing of the shofar commemorates Abraham's willingness to sacrifice his son Isaac and God's acceptance of a ram in place of Isaac.

Fishman, Cathy Goldberg. *On Rosh Hashanah and Yom Kippur.* New York: Aladdin Paperbacks, 2000. Unpaged. Illustrated by Melanie W. Hall. $5.99. ISBN 0-689-83892-1.

📖 PICTURE BOOK—Fiction; Jewish
Ages 5 and up

Summary

A little girl explains Rosh Hashanah and Yom Kippur, how she knows they are coming, what they mean, what her family does, what happens in the synagogue, and what kind of prayers are said. The book ends with a glossary of terms.

Booktalk

On Rosh Hashanah, we celebrate a new year. My brother calls it the world's birthday. My grandmother says Rosh Hashanah is the day God created the world. My mother says that means it is a new year for how we think and act. We celebrate Rosh Hashanah by sending cards to people we know, by eating special foods like challah bread and apples dipped in honey, and by going to the synagogue to pray. I throw my bad deeds and thoughts into the river and promise to do better in the next year.

Learning Extensions (Language Arts)

A new year is a time for new beginnings. Some celebrate with religious observances, others with parties and resolutions. Serve challah bread and apples dipped in honey. Ask children when and how their families celebrate a new year. Gather a collection of books about Rosh Hashanah, Chinese New Year, and the New Year that begins on January 1. Encourage children to read, then compare and contrast the observances. Older children may follow up with written or oral reports.

Kimmel, Eric A. *Gershon's Monster: A Story for the Jewish New Year.* New York: Scholastic, 2000. Unpaged. Illustrated by Jon J. Muth. $16.95. ISBN 0-439-10839-X.

📖 PICTURE BOOK—Fiction; Jewish
Ages 5–10

Summary

The author retells an early Hasidic legend from the region of Poland where his ancestors once lived.

Booktalk

Gershon is a proud and selfish man. He never does anything really bad, but he cares little about how he treats others. And he never, ever, says, "I'm sorry." Every Friday he sweeps his mistakes into the cellar. Once a year, he puts them into a sack and tosses them into the sea. Now Gershon and his wife want a child, so Gershon travels to the home of the wonder rabbi and insists that the rabbi ask God to send them a child. The rabbi gives Gershon a warning. Will the prophecy come true?

Learning Extensions (Character Education)

Follow up by reading the author's note that tells briefly of the origins of the legend, of Rosh Hashanah, and of the custom of tossing one's sins into the sea and that discusses the meaning of and lists the six steps of repentance. Engage children in a discussion of what it is to be sorry for one's mistakes and to return to one's best self.

Marx, David F. *Rosh Hashanah and Yom Kippur.* New York: Childrens Press, 2001. 31p. $5.95. ISBN 0-516-22266-X.

 📖 PICTURE BOOK—Nonfiction
 Ages 5–7

Summary

Photographs and simple text explain the history and celebration of Rosh Hashanah and Yom Kippur.

Read-Aloud

The short, simple text and full-page photographs lend themselves to reading aloud and showing the photographs.

Learning Extensions (Language Arts)

Invite the children to revisit the book by showing the pictures and asking them to retell what is happening in each picture.

Rau, Dana Meachen. *Rosh Hashanah and Yom Kippur.* New York: Childrens Press, 2001. 47p. $25.00. ISBN 0-516-22243-0.

📖 CHAPTER BOOK—Nonfiction
Ages 7–10

Summary

Full-color photographs augment the informative text that describes the holidays Rosh Hashanah and Yom Kippur, which celebrate the beginning of a new year.

Booktalk

The Jewish High Holy Days begin with Rosh Hashanah and end 10 days later with Yom Kippur. Rosh Hashanah is also called the Day of Remembering, the Day of Judgment, and the Day of Sounding the Shofar. Yom Kippur is called the Day of Atonement. What happens on these special days?

Learning Extensions (Character Education, Social Studies)

Have the children discuss the concepts of judgment and atonement. How do these ideas affect them? How have they affected groups of people in history? Is it good to use these concepts in political and social affairs? Or does it cause problems?

Other Books to Use for Rosh Hashanah

Holub, Joan. *Apples and Honey: A Rosh Hashanah Book.* New York: Puffin Books, 2003. Ages 4–8. 16p. Illustrated by Cary Pilo. $6.99. ISBN 0-142-501360.

Rouss, Sylvia. *Sammy Spider's First Rosh Hashanah.* Rockville, Md.: Kar-Ben Publishing, 1996. Ages 4–8. 32p. Illustrated by Katherine J. Kahn. $6.95. ISBN 0-929-371992.

11
October

INTRODUCTION

October is Diversity Awareness Month, a time to recognize and respect all people, including those with disabilities. Books selected for inclusion focus on children with disabilities. Chang does not speak but earns the money to buy his mother a new wok by playing his flute. A dance company performs with some dancers in wheelchairs. A hearing-impaired child and friends communicate using sign language. A little girl gets a speeding ticket for racing her wheelchair but saves her brother by rushing him to the hospital.

Columbus Day celebrates the anniversary of Christopher Columbus's arrival in the New World. Readers will meet Christopher Columbus as well as the first people who traveled to America across the land bridge from Asia and 12-year-old Diego Bermudez, who sailed as a page with Columbus.

140 ■ *October*

Three holidays fall at the end of October: Diwali, which is the Hindu Festival of Lights; Dia de los Muertos, which is Mexico's Day of the Dead; and Halloween. Children will have opportunities to respond with choral reading, by discussing open-ended questions, by making a Fraidy Cat Safe Halloween book, and other activities related to language arts, social studies, character education, developing research skills, art, music and dance, and even Spanish.

11.1 DIVERSITY AWARENESS MONTH

The purpose of Diversity Awareness Month is to foster an understanding and appreciation of all people regardless of culture, race, gender, sexual preference, or disability. The observance was recently established around 2000.

Elizabeth Starr Hill. *Chang and the Bamboo Flute.* New York: Farrar, Straus & Giroux, 2002. 60p. Illustrated by Lesley Lui. $15.00. ISBN 0-374-31238-9.

  CHAPTER BOOK—Fiction; Chinese; Mute
  Ages 7–10

Summary

Heavy rains cause the river to flood and damage the houseboat where Chang, who is mute, and his parents live. After the waters subside, Chang's mother discovers that her wonderful wok is missing. Chang earns the money to buy a new wok by playing his flute. (This novella is a sequel to *Bird Boy,* the first book about Chang, which is written for the same age range.)

Booktalk

Chang lives with his parents on a houseboat on the river. When heavy rains come, they destroy the crops in the fields and cause the river to rise. As the river floods the land upstream, debris begins to tumble down the river toward Chang's houseboat. Then it happens! The wheel of a wooden cart hits the side of the boat, tearing part of the cabin away, and water rushes in.. What will happen to Chang and his parents?

Learning Extensions (Language Arts, Character Education)

Divide the children into two groups. Present one group with this question: How did Jinan and Zhao hurt Chang's feelings and cause him to feel discouraged? Present the other group with this question: How did the friendship of Mei Mei and Bo Won help Chang? Have the first group list on a chart how Jinan and Zhao hurt and discouraged Chang. Have the other group list on a chart how Mei Mei and Bo Won helped Chang. Then have the children discuss whether they would like to be friends with Jinan and Zhao or with Mei Mei and Bo Won. Be sure to ask the children to explain why they would like to be friends with Jinan and Zhao or Mei Mei and Bo Won. Finally, ask the children to think about how they treat others who are different from them. Do they act like Jinan and Zhao or like Mei Mei and Bo Won?

McMahon, Patricia. *Dancing Wheels.* Boston: Houghton Mifflin, 2000. 48p. Photographs by John Godt. $16.00. ISBN 0-395-88889-1.

 PICTURE BOOK—Nonfiction; Photo Essay; Physically Limited
Ages 9 and up

Summary

Dancing Wheels is the name of a dance company comprised of stand-up and sit-down dancers. The sit-down dancers are in wheelchairs. Mary Verdi-Fletcher, founder of the dance company, decided at the age of four that she wanted to become a dancer even though she was born with spina bifida. This book shows how young dancers put on a show after practicing and working together.

Booktalk

Mary Verdi-Fletcher has a dream—a big dream She wants to become a dancer. But Mary has braces on her legs, and she often sits in a wheelchair. You see, Mary had been born with spina bifida, a congenital malformation of the spinal cord. Nevertheless, Mary eventually becomes a dancer. She even founds a dance company. Learn more about this amazing person and her inspiring life in *Dancing Wheels.*

Learning Extensions (Music and Dance)

Ask the children if any of them dance. Ask if they have danced with sit-down dancers. Engage the entire group in a discussion of dancing, what it is, and how to dance in a chair. Like Sabatino, the dance teacher, have children listen to the sounds, rhythms, and songs of their names. Have each child dance his or her name by using his or her head, arms, hands, and body. Then select a simple story, such as a folktale or a fairy tale, that all children know. Have children select parts, plan their movements, and retell the story by dancing. Have some children be stand-up dancers and others be sit-down dancers.

Millman, Isaac. *Moses Goes to a Concert.* New York: Farrar, Straus & Giroux, 1998. Unpaged. $5.95. ISBN 0-374-45366-7.

 📖 PICTURE BOOK—Fiction; Hearing Impaired
   Ages 5–8

Summary

Moses and his classmates, who are all hearing impaired, attend a music concert with their teacher. Sign language diagrams showing short sentences and phrases are interspersed throughout the book. The book ends with two pages of sign language diagrams with which Moses tells his parents about the concerts. The last page shows hand-spelling diagrams.

Booktalk

Moses and his classmates are hearing impaired. They cannot hear—or not as well as other children. They are going to a concert with their teacher. Their teacher is deaf, and so is the percussionist who plays in the orchestra. How will Moses, his classmates, and their teacher hear the concert? How does the percussionist hear the music and know when and how to play her instruments?

Learning Extensions (Music)

Provide musical experiences like the ones that Moses and his classmates enjoyed. For a playing experience, provide children with an assortment of percussion instruments, such as drums, bells, and triangles. Tell children to take off their shoes, then give each child an instrument. Tell children to feel the vibrations in their feet as they play their instruments. For a listening experience, give each child a balloon. Tell children to hold the balloons on their laps to feel the music as did Moses and his classmates. Then play music of your choice for the children to listen to. A second response is to develop simple sign language skills by using the directions and diagrams in the book.

Munsch, Robert. *Zoom!* New York: Scholastic, 2003. 30p. Illustrated by Michael Martchenko. $13.95. ISBN 0-439-18774-5.

    PICTURE BOOK—Fiction; Physically Limited
Ages 5–8

Summary

Lauretta gets a new wheelchair and a speeding ticket and saves her brother by rushing him to the hospital.

Booktalk

How can a kid in a wheelchair get a speeding ticket? Lauretta did! Her wheelchair is brand new. It is black, silver, and red, and it has 92 gears. Even after the speeding ticket, Lauretta said her new wheelchair was too slow. What does that girl want?

Learning Extensions (Language Arts, Art)

Have the children write newspaper articles based on events in the book (such as news stories about Lauretta's speeding ticket, her brother's accident, and her rush to the hospital with her brother) or advertisements for Lauretta's wheelchairs. Some children might want to draw cartoons and write balloon dialogue about Lauretta testing the wheelchairs.

Other Books to Use for Diversity Awareness

Cohen, Peter, and Olof Landstrom. *Boris's Glasses*. Stockholm: R&S Books, 2003. Ages 6–9. Unpaged. $15.00. ISBN 91-29-65942-6.

Denenberg, Barry. *Mirror, Mirror on the Wall: The Diary of Bess Brennan, the Perkins School for the Blind, 1932*. New York: Scholastic, 2002. Ages 9–14. 144p. $10.95. ISBN 0-439-19446-6.

Matlin, Marlee. *Deaf Child Crossing*. New York: Aladdin Paperbacks, 2004. Ages 8–12. 200p. $4.99. ISBN 0-689-86696-8.

11.2 COLUMBUS DAY

Columbus Day is the anniversary of Christopher Columbus's arrival in the New World. Since 1971, Columbus Day has been observed on the second Monday of October as a federal holiday, which means that banks, post offices, and government offices are closed. The first recorded celebration of Columbus Day in the United States occurred on October 12, 1792, the 300th anniversary of Columbus's arrival in the New World. President Benjamin Harrison declared the first official Columbus Day holiday in 1892, the 400th anniversary of his arrival. By 1920, Columbus Day was celebrated annually. President Franklin Roosevelt declared October 12 as the official holiday in 1937. President Lyndon Johnson moved the holiday to the second Monday in October and declared it a federal holiday.

Many prefer that Columbus Day be celebrated as Indigenous Peoples' Day because Christopher Columbus was not the first to discover America, nor was he the first European to land in the New World. Rather, he was the first European to conquer America's native people. Therefore, many prefer to celebrate America's native people on this day.

Ansary, Mir Tamim. *Columbus*. Des Plaines, Ill.: Heinemann Library, 1999. 32p. ISBN 1-57572-702-1.

 📖 PICTURE BOOK—Nonfiction
  Ages 7–10

Summary

Color photographs, maps, and simple text explain the history of migration and then describe Columbus's voyage to the New World and the European development that followed.

Bookwalk

Use the maps on pages 8, 13, and 25 to explain that the first people to come to America traveled across the land bridge that once connected Asia to North America (map, page 8). Many years later, Europeans traveled to the Indies for spices and silk (map, page 13). Columbus believed that he could reach the Indies by sailing west. Instead of reaching the Indies, Columbus reached the islands lying off the coast of North and South America (map, page 25) and changed the course of history.

Learning Extensions (Social Studies, Research Skills)

Using the map on page 25, have children identify the 23 new countries that were developed in North and South America. Organize the children in small groups or in pairs. Have each group or pair identify a country or countries in a specific portion of the map. Then have the groups or pairs research and report on Columbus Day celebrations in the countries that they identified.

Hoose, Phillip. "'Tierra!' When Two Worlds Met." In *We Were There, Too!* (pp. 2–11). New York: Farrar, Straus & Giroux, 2001. 264p. $26.00. ISBN 0-374-38252-2.

 PICTURE BOOK—Nonfiction
Ages 10 and up

Summary

"'Tierra!' When Two Worlds Met," tells of 12-year-old Diego Bermudez, who sailed with Columbus aboard the *Santa Maria,* and of the Tainos who greeted Columbus when he landed in the New World. Sidebars provide additional related information.

Booktalk

If you think grown-ups are the only ones who can have adventures, think again. Diego Bermudez was only 12 years old when he sailed to America with Columbus. He sailed as a page. A page did the work that no one else wanted to do, like cook hot meals, scrub blackened pots, and clean the deck. Many young boys sailed on ships in those days. The Tainos, native people who greeted Columbus when he landed in the New World, were a young people too. Columbus reported that about half the Tainos were under the age of 15 years.

Read more about the youngsters who sailed with Columbus and the Tainos who greeted them when they arrived in the New World.

Learning Extensions (Social Studies, Research Skills)

Have children do research about the boys who sailed with Columbus and about the Tainos by using references listed in the back of the book and searching Web sites such as The Columbus Navigation Homepage at www1.minn.net/~keithp, www.geocities.com/columbus_website, and www.surfnetkind.com/columbus.htm.

Other Books to Use for Columbus Day

Ganeri, Anita. *The Story of Columbus.* New York: Dorling-Kindersley Books, 2001. Ages 7–10. 32p. $12.95. ISBN 0-789-478773.

Roop, Peter, and Connie Roop. *Christopher Columbus.* New York: Scholastic, 2000. Ages 8–12. 128p. $12.95. ISBN 0-439-271800.

Sundel, Al. *Christopher Columbus and the Age of Exploration in World History.* Berkeley Heights, N.J.: Enslow Publishers, 2002. Ages 8–12. 128p. $26.60. ISBN 0-766-018202.

11.3 DIWALI

Diwali is the five-day Hindu Festival of Lights, which falls in late October or early November on the fifteenth day of the Hindu month of Ashwin. Diwali has its origins in prehistoric times as a festive celebration of the harvest and beginning of the new year. Myths, legends, beliefs, and celebrations vary with different regions. But common to all are sweets, fireworks, and the practice of lighting every home with lamps.

Gardeski, Christina Mia. *Diwali.* New York: Childrens Press, 2001. 31p. $5.95. ISBN 0-516-22372-0.

 📖 PICTURE BOOK—Nonfiction; Hindu
Ages 5–7

Summary

Photographs and simple text explain the history and celebration of Diwali.

Read-Aloud

The short, simple text and color photographs lend themselves to reading aloud and showing the photographs.

Learning Extensions (Language Arts)

Invite the children to revisit the book by showing the pictures and asking them to retell what is happening in each picture.

Kacker, Anisha. *Ravi's Diwali Surprise.* Cleveland: Modern Curriculum Press, 1994. 23p. Illustrated by Kusum Ohri. $12.95. ISBN 0-8136-2334-0.

  PICTURE BOOK—Fiction; Hindu
  Ages 7–12

Summary

Ravi and his family prepare to celebrate Diwali in their home near New Jersey.

Booktalk

It is October, and Ravi is in the kitchen helping his mother prepare for Diwali. Diwali is a happy feast, but Ravi doesn't feel very happy as he thinks about his older brother, Shankar. Shankar hasn't called or written since he left for college. Shankar and Ravi always put the lights up together for Diwali. Ayushi and her family are coming in time for the evening prayer service, but will Shankar be here? And will he come in time to put up the lights?

Learning Extensions (Language Arts)

Invite the children to share what they know about Hinduism and India. Encourage them to ask questions and to identify what they want to learn more about, such as foods, the story of Prince Ram, the use of lights, shrines, Lakshmi, and Ganesh. Use the books that are reviewed in chapter 13, "Holidays in General: Indian Cultures" for more information.

Other Books to Use for Diwali

Gilmour, Rachna. *Lights for Gita.* Gardiner, Me.: Tilbury House, 1994. Ages 4–8. Unpaged. Illustrated by Alice Priestley. $9.95. ISBN 0-884-481514.

Zucker, Jonny. *Lighting a Lamp: A Diwali Story.* Hauppauge, N.Y.: Barron's Educational Series, 2004. Ages 4–8. 24p. $6.95. ISBN 0-764-126709.

11.4 DAY OF THE DEAD

Day of the Dead, Dia de los Muertos, is a three-day Mexican holiday that runs from October 31 to November 2. Day of the Dead, based on Aztec and Christian origins, is a festive celebration that honors the dead. Aztecs believed that the souls of the dead return to their homes once a year at the end of July and early August. Christians honor their faithful departed on November 1, the feast of All Saints, and on November 2, the feast of All Souls. Spanish priests moved the Aztec celebration to late October and early November to fall on Halloween, the feast of All Saints, and the feast of All Souls.

Families celebrate Day of the Dead by placing food, marigolds, candles, incense, mementos, photos, and other remembrances on their altars at home, by picnicking in the cemetery at the graves of their departed, and by telling stories about their loved ones. Special foods such as breads, fruits, vegetables, and sweets; papier-mâché and sugar skulls, cardboard coffins; masks; and tissue banner decorations add to the festivities.

Freschet, Gina. *Beto and the Bone Dance.* New York: Farrar, Straus & Giroux, 2001. Unpaged. $16.00. ISBN 0-374-31720-8.

 📖 PICTURE BOOK—Fiction; Mexican
 Ages 5–8

Summary

This is the story of a little boy and his family who celebrate Halloween in Mexico. In Mexico, Halloween is called Dia de los Muertos, Day of the Dead.

Booktalk

Beto loves Day of the Dead. That's when skulls and skeletons decorate the town. Beto loves to help his family decorate an altar for his dead grandmother with her favorite foods and flowers. Even better, he loves to parade from house to house singing for bread and chocolate. What could be more fun than staying up all night, picnicking at the cemetery, listening to the strolling musicians, telling stories, and watching the fireworks. But this year, a skeleton pulls Beto into the dance, and that's when the fun begins!

Learning Extensions (Spanish, Research Skills)

Have children practice some Spanish words and phrases then use this book to launch a discussion of the history and customs of Halloween. Visit www.spooky-halloween.com for more information about Day of the Dead, which is of Aztec origin; about the Celtic roots of Halloween; and about other history and customs related to Halloween.

Lasky, Kathryn. *Days of the Dead.* New York: Hyperion Books for Children, 1994. 48p. Photographs by Christopher G. Knight. $16.49. ISBN 0-7868-2018-7.

📖 PICTURE BOOK—Nonfiction
Ages 8–12

Summary

Color photographs supplement the detailed text that explains Day of the Dead and describes how Gamaliel and his family celebrate in their valley. More information about Day of the Dead, All Saints' Day and All Souls' Day, Halloween, and Egyptian festivals honoring the dead is given in the back of the book.

Booktalk

At the end of October, many of us celebrate Halloween. Some call it All Saints' Day or All Souls' Day. But 12-year-old Gamaliel and his family, who live on a farm in a valley outside Mexico City, celebrate Day of the Dead. This is a happy time of rejoicing and celebrating. How do Gamaliel and his family celebrate? Learn about the special celebrations of this Mexican holiday in *Days of the Dead*.

Learning Extensions (Language Arts)

Encourage children to share the ways in which their families honor and remember their loved ones who have died. Some may observe

All Saints' Day and All Souls' Day. Others may visit cemeteries on Memorial Day or at other times of the year. Still other families may have pictures, tell stories, and even have family histories or genealogies.

Wade, Mary Dodson. *El Dia de los Muertos: The Day of the Dead.* New York: Childrens Press, 2002. 31p. $19.50. ISBN 0-516-22493.

 EASY READER—Nonfiction
 Ages 5–8

Summary

Color photographs and simple text describe the celebration of Day of the Dead, the day when Mexican families remember their loved ones who have died.

Read-Aloud

Before reading, engage children in a discussion of what Day of the Dead might be. Then tell children to listen while you read aloud to find out.

Learning Extensions (Language Arts)

After reading, have the children to take turns retelling what they heard. Prompt them by asking open-ended questions such as the following: "Now who can tell us what Day of the Dead is?" Encourage other children to add to what has been said by asking, "What else did you learn about Day of the Dead? Can anyone add to what has been said?" Probe for more information by asking open-ended questions such as the following: "How did families celebrate? Where did they go? What did they do? What did they eat?"

Other Books to Use for Day of the Dead

Johnston, Tony. *Day of the Dead.* San Diego: Harcourt Brace, 1997. Ages 4–8. Unpaged. Illustrated by Jeanette Winter. $6.00. ISBN 0-152-228632.

San Vincente, Luis. *Festival of the Bones.* El Paso, Tex.: Cinco Puntas Press, 2002. Ages 4–8. 32p. $14.95. ISBN 0-938-317679.

11.5 HALLOWEEN

Halloween falls on October 31, the eve of All Saints' Day, and was known in medieval times as All Hallows Eve. October 31 is also the Celtic festival of Samhain celebrating the end of summer, the harvest, and protection of crops and herds from wandering evil spirits. The Celtic and Anglo-Saxon new year begins November 1. In the late nineteenth century, Irish immigrants introduced Halloween customs to the United States. Mischief making, such as overturning outhouses and breaking windows, became widespread. In Scotland, a turnip was used as a jack-o'-lantern. The pumpkin replaced the turnip in the United States, and small children going from door to door for "trick or treat" replaced the earlier mischief making.

Freymann, Saxton, and Joost Elffers. *Dr. Pompo's Nose.* New York: Scholastic, 2000. Unpaged. $15.95. ISBN 0-439-11013-0.

    PICTURE BOOK—Fiction
    Ages 5–8

Summary

Dr. Pompo and his pumpkin friends have different ideas about what the mysterious something on the floor might be. It is Ms. Sniffens's pumpkin nose.

Booktalk

Show the picture on the left page of the first two-page spread while covering the picture on the right page so that children cannot see what it is. Then say, "Dr. Pompo has found something on the floor. But what is it?" Dr. Pompo asks each of his pumpkin friends—is it a gardening tool, a sheep-calling horn, a horn from a goat's head, a horn for hearing, a dinosaur fossil? Finally, Mrs. Sniffens solves the mystery. What do you suppose the mysterious something might be?

Learning Extensions (Language Arts)

Read aloud and show the pictures. Before you read each page, ask the children to predict what the mysterious something might be and then ask what else it might be. When you finish reading, serve roasted pumpkin seeds. Ask, "Why are pumpkins used at Halloween time?" Discuss the origins of this custom.

Heller, Nicholas, *Elwood and the Witch*. New York: Greenwillow Books, 2000. Unpaged. Illustrated by Joseph A. Smith. $15.95. ISBN 0-688-16945-7.

   PICTURE BOOKS—Fiction
   Ages 5 and up

Summary

Elwood finds a broom leaning against a tree—a witch's broom. As he flies over the treetops, the witch discovers he's riding her broom, becomes angry, and fires spells at him. The moon saves Elwood by telling the witch to listen and telling Elwood how to land.

Booktalk

Elwood finds a witch's broom leaning against a tree. That's when his adventures begin. Instead of sweeping his front step, the broom takes Elwood for a ride over the treetops. Now the witch discovers that Elwood is riding her broom. She fires spells at him. But she doesn't know that Elwood doesn't know how to land!

Learning Extensions (Language Arts)

Retell the story by following the pictures and talking about the action depicted in the pictures. Although it is not a Halloween story, this story is appropriate to read for Halloween. Engage children in a discussion of what happens when we get angry and don't listen to what the other person is saying.

Larranaga, Ana Martin. *Woo! The Not-So-Scary Ghost*. New York: Arthur A. Levine Books, 2000. Unpaged. $15.95. ISBN 0-439-16958-5.

   PICTURE BOOK—Fiction
   Ages 3–7

Summary

This simple picture book with limited text tells about the little ghost who isn't scary.

Read-Aloud

Woo, the little ghost, isn't very scary. He runs away, only to discover that no one is afraid of him: not the dog, the farmer, the goat, or the kittens. Read aloud and show the pictures.

Learning Extensions (Art, Language Arts)

Make "ghost" hand puppets from white paper. Make patterns by having children trace the outlines of their hands. Have them turn their hands over and trace their thumbs on the other side of the outline to make the second "ghost" arm. Cut, then make a handle by gluing a popsicle stick or tongue depressor to the back. Ask children for suggestions as to what Woo can do to be scary. Act out being a scary ghost using the hand puppets. Follow up by showing the video *Caspar Meets Wendy*.

Patschke, Steve. *The Spooky Book*. New York: Walker & Co., 1999. Unpaged. Illustrated by Matthew McElligott. $15.95. ISBN 0-8027-8692-8.

 PICTURE BOOK—Fiction
 Ages 5–8

Summary

This is a book within a book within a book about a boy and girl who each read a scary book about the other.

Booktalk

Andrew reads a spooky book about a girl named ZoZo, who is reading a spooky book about a boy who is alone in a spooky house. When Andrew hears knocking on his door, he becomes very, very frightened. Who do you suppose is there?

Learning Extensions (Language Arts)

Read aloud, showing the pictures. Have the children plan and engage in choral reading with the boys reading Andrew's part and the girls reading ZoZo's part.

Teague, Mark. *One Halloween Night*. New York: Scholastic, 1999. Unpaged. $14.95. ISBN 0-590-84625-6.

📖 **PICTURE BOOK**—Fiction
Ages 5–9

Summary

In this Halloween adventure filled with trouble from the start, Wendell, Floyd, and Mona turn the tables on Leola and her witch friends.

Booktalk

Wendell, Floyd, and Mona have nothing but trouble on Halloween. And the trouble only gets worse as the night wears on. Even the treats turn into tricks. Is it the black cat that crossed their path? Then Wendell produces a magic potion, and Mona uses her magic wand.

Learning Extensions (Art, Language Arts)

Make a Fraidy Cat Safe Halloween book by cutting a cat shape for the book and writing safety tips for Halloween.

Other Books to Use for Halloween

Diviny, Sean. *Halloween Motel.* New York: HarperCollins, 2000. Ages 4–8. Unpaged. Illustrated by Joe Rocco. $15.95. ISBN 0-06-028815-9.

Minor, Wendell. *Pumpkin Heads!* New York: Blue Sky Press, 2000. Ages 4–8. Unpaged. $15.95. ISBN 0-590-52105-5.

Page, Jason. *Whamboozle.* New York: William Morrow & Co., 1999. Ages 4–8. Unpaged. Illustrated by Sebastian Quigley. $11.95. ISBN 0-688-17175-3.

12
November

INTRODUCTION

November is National American Indian Heritage Month, a time to honor and recognize America's original peoples. The books chosen for National American Indian Heritage Month are intended to reflect the diversity of America's original peoples. One tells of the Navajo code talkers who successfully prevented the Japanese from intercepting and translating military messages during World War II. Another weaves together traditional Seneca legends. A third retells the daily life of the Algonquian Indians, while a fourth tells a story about the rock art left by the Anasazi Indians of the Southwest. Finally, a fifth tells about encounters between Florida's Indians (Timucua, Calusa, and Apalachee) and early Spanish and French explorers.

Election Day, Veterans' Day, and Thanksgiving also fall in November. Children will learn about women's struggle for the right to vote and how Duck became President; learn about World War II, the youngest U.S. soldier in the twentieth century, and a young soldier in Vietnam; and then learn some Thanksgiving knock-knock jokes and enjoy some Thanksgiving chuckles with the Know-Nothings. Suggested responses include creating paper sculptures, planning a mock election, making Veterans' Day thank-you cards to give to veterans, and other activities related to social studies, language arts, and the development of critical thinking and research skills.

12.1 NATIONAL AMERICAN INDIAN HERITAGE MONTH

In 1990, President George Bush proclaimed November National American Indian Heritage Month. Its purpose is to honor and recognize America's original peoples. The first American Indian Day was celebrated in 1916. In 1976, Native American Awareness Week was held October 10–16.

Aaseng, Nathan. *Navajo Code Talkers: America's Secret Weapon in World War II.* New York: Walker & Co., 2000. 114p. $8.95. ISBN 0-8027-7589-6.

 CHAPTER BOOK—Nonfiction
 Ages 9–12

Summary

During World War II, the U.S. Marine Corps recruited young Navajo men to serve as radio operators in the Pacific theater. A military code using the Navajo language was developed for transmitting messages. The Navajo code talkers successfully prevented the Japanese from intercepting and translating military messages.

Booktalk

During World War II, the U.S. Marines desperately needed a secret code—an unbreakable code that they could use to transmit radio messages in the Pacific without the Japanese military understanding them. A civilian and engineer, Philip Johnston, the son of Protestant missionaries to the Navajo, came up with an idea. Fluent in the Navajo language, Philip knew how difficult it was. Johnston met with a signal officer from Camp Elliott in southern California and suggested that a military code based on the Navajo language be created. That was the beginning of the Navajo code talkers, who played a significant role in the war in the Pacific and became heroes.

Learning Extensions (Social Studies, Research Skills, Language Arts)

After reading the book, have children form four groups. Have each group select a topic: the Navajo Code Talkers, Navajo Culture,

World War II Cryptography, and World War II Battles—Pacific. Use the references cited in the bibliography as well as other sources to research and report on their topics.

Martin, Rafe. *The World Before This One.* New York: Arthur A. Levine Books, 2002. 208p. $16.95. ISBN 0-590-37976-3.

 📖 CHAPTER BOOK—Fiction
 Ages 10 and up

Summary

The author weaves a selection of traditional Seneca legends into the unified story of the young Indian boy, Crow, who learns the stories from the long ago from Grandfather Stone, a talking rock located deep in the forest.

Booktalk

Grandmother fears that some sort of evil power prevents Crow from finding the birds they need to eat. She sends Crow's trusted friend Raccoon as a spy to follow Crow into the forest and report back to her about what he sees. Raccoon says only that the birds are hard to find. Is that true? Raccoon is Crow's friend. Perhaps he is not telling her everything. Grandmother asks Raccoon's father to follow the boys with his warriors. Like Raccoon, Eagle and his warriors say only that the birds were hard to find. What is behind this? Crow has his father's power to hunt. Why are the birds so hard to find?

Learning Extensions (Language Arts, Art)

Use the sources cited in the author's note to read and retell other versions of the Seneca tales incorporated in this book. Have the children use the paper sculpture illustrations as a model for creating their own paper sculptures.

McCurdy, Michael. *An Algonquian Year: The Year According to the Full Moon.* Boston: Houghton Mifflin, 2000. Unpaged. $15.00. ISBN 0-618-00705-9.

    📖 PICTURE BOOK—Nonfiction
    Ages 6–10

Summary

Twelve two-page spreads, one for each month of the year, retell the daily life of the Algonquian Indians. A full-page scratchboard illustration enlivens each facing page of text.

Read-Aloud

Read the introduction that tells about the Algonquian people. Continue to read about each month and tell a little about it as depicted in the illustration.

Learning Extensions (Social Studies)

Use the bibliography in the back of the book to learn more about the Algonquian tribes, such as the Micmacs, Wampanoags, and Abenakis.

Taylor, Harriet Peck. *Secrets of the Stone.* New York: Farrar, Straus & Giroux, 2000. Unpaged. $16.00. ISBN 0-374-36648-9.

    📖 PICTURE BOOK—Fiction
    Ages 6–10

Summary

Stylized illustrations enhance the tale of Coyote and Badger, who discover ancient rock art on the walls of a cave as they chase Jackrabbit into a hole. Traditional designs border each page of text. An author's note and sources at the end of the book provide more information about the ancient rock art.

Bookwalk

Open the book to the first two-page spread and tell the children that Coyote and Badger hunted together in the desert that was their home. Turn the page, show the picture, and tell the children that Coyote and Badger cornered Jackrabbit, who slipped away through a hole. Continue paging through the book, telling the story.

Learning Extensions (Social Studies, Art)

Use the sources cited in the back of the book to learn more about the rock art left by the Anasazi Indians of the Southwest. Older children might research other ancient cultures that left rock art.

Weitzel, Kelley G. *Journeys with Florida's Indians*. Gainesville: University Press of Florida, 2002. 228p. $24.95. ISBN 0-8130-2581-8.

 📖 CHAPTER BOOK—Nonfiction and Fiction
 Ages 9–14

Summary

The author alternates fiction with nonfiction, incorporating storytelling through the fictional character Tenerife to tell stories about Florida's Indians: the Timucua, Calusa, and Apalachee. The book begins with the arrival of the first people in Florida and concludes with the impact of the Spanish and French explorers on native cultures. Drawings, engravings, and maps supplement the text. The book begins with a chronology of important events and ends with a glossary, references, and a list of Native American places to visit.

Booktalk

Fire! Fire! Now is their chance to escape. Tenerife, a Timucua Indian boy, and his friend Sheko, an African slave, silently slip into a canoe and paddle up the Tocobaga River. The two leave behind the land of the Calusas, but who knows what the Tocobagas might do! Tenerife and Sheko hide their canoe when they hear other people. They fish and live off the land as they make their way northeast toward Tenerife's home, until one night, as they sit by their fire, the Challenger walks into their camp. Who is he? And what will he do?

Learning Extensions (Social Studies, Critical Thinking)

Have the children use a map of Florida and the Caribbean to retrace Tenerife's journeys. Construct a time line and record the significant events that occurred If you and your children live in Florida, select from the list of Native American places to visit in the back of the book a place near you for a field trip. If not, use the addresses, telephone numbers, or e-mail addresses that are provided to obtain more information about places of interest to you and your children.

Other Books to Use for Native American Heritage Month

Bruchac, Joseph. *Many Nations.* New York: Cartwheel Books, 2004. Ages 4–8. 32p. Illustrated by Robert F. Goetzl. $5.99. ISBN 0-439-63590-X.

Curry, Jane Louise. *Hold Up the Sky and Other Native American Tales from Texas and the Southern Plains.* New York: Margaret K. McElderry Books, 2003. Ages 8–12. 154p. Illustrated by James Watts. $17.95. ISBN 0-689-85287-8.

Vaughan, Marcia. *Night Dancer: Mythical Piper of the Native American Southwest.* New York: Orchard Books, 2002. Ages 6–10. Unpaged. Illustrated by Lisa Desimini. $16.95. ISBN 0-439-35248-7.

12.2 ELECTION DAY

Election Day, the day American voters cast their votes for the presidential electors who form the Electoral College, occurs every four years on the Tuesday after the first Monday in November. The number of electors for each state is at least three, is based on population, and is equal to the number of the state's congressional delegates. The Electoral College then meets on the first Tuesday after the second Wednesday in December to elect the president and vice president. Congress established Election Day in 1854, choosing early November out of consideration for the farmers who had to reap their harvests. Tuesday was chosen so that people who had to travel could do so on Monday rather than Sunday.

Cronin Doreen. *Duck for President.* New York: Simon & Schuster Books for Young Readers, 2004. Unpaged. Illustrated by Betsy Lewin. $15.95. ISBN 0-689-86377-2.

 📖 PICTURE BOOK—Fiction
 All Ages

Summary

Duck was unhappy doing chores, so he campaigned to be elected farmer. Unhappy running the farm, Duck campaigned to be elected governor—and then president.

Booktalk

Duck didn't like doing chores, running the farm, or even being the state governor. Do you suppose he'll be happy running the country as president?

Learning Extensions (Social Studies)

Have children plan and hold a mock election. Use the book as a guide. First of all, decide what office candidates are running for, such as class president, running the library, or running the school. Decide what the requirements are to vote, then register all voters. Decide and post election issues. Nominate candidates and have each candidate campaign for office by making posters, holding meetings, and giving speeches. Then vote and count all ballots. Announce the winner of the election.

Hoose, Phillip. "Edna Purtell: Suffragist." In *We Were There, Too! Young People in U.S. History* (pp. 181–183). New York.: Farrar, Straus & Giroux, 2001. 264p. $26.00. ISBN 0-374-388252-2.

 PICTURE BOOK—Nonfiction
 Ages 10 and up

Summary

The account of Edna Purtell tells of one teenager's experiences as she struggles for women's right to vote.

Booktalk

She was only 16, but Edna Purtell was already recognized as a leader among women. Why? When the mother of actress Katherine Hepburn offered to pay Edna's way to a demonstration in Washington, D.C., Edna immediately agreed. She was jailed four times during that demonstration. Other women demonstrated, spoke out, and fought; some even died—all for the right to vote.

Learning Extensions (Social Studies, Research Skills)

Encourage students to learn more about women's struggle for the right to vote and some of the women who led the struggle. Why were they called "suffragettes"? Research the women's suffrage movement in the library and on the Internet. How long did it take American women to win the right to vote? A sidebar notes that the constitutional amendment granting women the right to vote was first introduced in the U.S. Congress in 1878 and was reintroduced every year until it was finally adopted in 1920. Another sidebar notes that Wyoming granted women the right to vote in 1869.

McNamara, Margaret. *Robin Hill School: Election Day.* New York: First Aladdin Paperbacks, 2004. 32p. Illustrated by Mike Gordon. $3.99. ISBN 0-689-86425-6.

 BEGINNING CHAPTER BOOK
 Ages 4–6

Summary

Mrs. Connor's class elects Becky to be their new class president.

Booktalk

It is election day in Mrs. Connor's class. The candidates for class president give speeches. Nick promises a candy machine. Emma promises no homework. Nia promises a six-month summer vacation. Becky promises to do her best. Who is elected the new class president?

Learning Extensions (Social Studies)

Ask the children who they would vote for as class president and why and ask if they were in Mrs. Connor's class.

Weiss, Ellen. *Hitty's Travels: Voting Rights Days.* New York: Aladdin Paperbacks, 2002. 75p. Illustrated by Betina Ogden. $3.99. ISBN 0-689-84912-5.

 BEGINNING CHAPTER BOOK
 Ages 6–9

Summary

Hitty is the doll given to Emily for Christmas. Emily lived in Washington, D.C., where her aunt and other women were jailed for demonstrating for the right to vote. More about the right to vote is included in the back of the book.

Booktalk

When Emily went with her mother and sister, Maria, to watch Aunt Ada and other women march for the right to vote in front of the White House, she took her doll Hitty. Emily also took Hitty when she went with her mother and sister to take food to Aunt Ada and the other women as they picketed the White House. That's how Hitty got her picture in the paper. Hitty even got a letter in the paper after Aunt Ada was arrested and put into jail. That's why Emily's mother ordered a new hat for Hitty.

Learning Extensions (Social Studies)

The Nineteenth Amendment, which gave women the right to vote, was passed on August 26, 1920. Have the children find a copy of that amendment and read what it actually says.

Another Book to Use for Election Day

Brown, Don. *A Voice from the Wilderness: The Story of Anna Howard Shaw.* Boston: Houghton Mifflin, 2001. Ages 7–10. Unpaged. $16.00. ISBN 0-618-08362-6.

12.3 VETERANS' DAY

Veterans' Day, November 11, was originally known as Armistice Day, the anniversary of the end of World War I. The armistice between the Allies and Germany was signed on November 11, 1918. In 1954, the name Armistice Day was changed to Veterans' Day. The day became an occasion to honor veterans from all wars and is celebrated with naturalization ceremonies, parades, speeches, laying of flowers on servicemen's graves, and special services at the Tomb of the Unknown Soldier in Arlington National Cemetery in Arlington, Virginia.

Ambrose, Stephen E. *The Good Fight: How World War II Was Won.* New York: Atheneum Books for Young Readers, 2001. 96p. $19.95. ISBN 0-689-84361-5.

 📖 PICTURE BOOK—Nonfiction
   All Ages

Summary

This photo-essay chronicles World War II from its origins in Europe and Asia through its major battles in Europe, Asia, the Pacific and the Atlantic, Africa, and the Aleutian Islands; to V-E and V-J Days, the war crimes trials, and the Marshall Plan. A time line of significant events from 1933 to 1945 is also included. The book concludes with a glossary, a bibliography, related Web sites, and an index.

Bookwalk

Show children the book's endpapers with the time line. Tell the children that events leading to World War II began in 1933 when Hitler became chancellor of Germany, although the war did not actually begin until Germany invaded Poland in 1939. The United States entered the war when Japan bombed Pearl Harbor in 1941. The war continued until first Germany and then Japan surrendered in 1945. Then turn to the maps on pages 8, 9, and 37. Show and explain the extent of the war in Europe, in the Pacific, and in China–Burma–India. Randomly show some of the full-page photographs in the book and tell the children that major events of the war are retold.

Learning Extensions (Social Studies, Language Arts)

Use a world map to locate and place the maps that are in the book. Using a world map will enable children to see why World War II is called a world war. Invite family, friends, and community members to share their experiences of the war. (Most of the World War II veterans are in their late 70s and 80s now. Those who were children and adolescents are in their late 60s and 70s.) Ask them to identify places and times that children can locate on the map. Use the time line on the endpapers to locate times. Encourage children to use the Web sites in the back of the book to research and report on additional information.

Hoose, Phillip. "Calvin Graham: Too Young to Be a Hero?": In *We Were There, Too! Young People in U.S. History* (pp. 202–204). New York: Farrar, Straus & Giroux, 2001. 264p. $26.00. ISBN 0-374-388252-2.

📖 PICTURE BOOK—Nonfiction
Ages 10 and up

Summary

Calvin Graham, at the age of 12, served during World War II and was the youngest U.S. soldier in the twentieth century.

Booktalk

Calvin Graham became one of our country's youngest veterans after he served in World War II. He received the Purple Heart, the Bronze Star, and several other medals. Amazingly, he was only 13 years old.

Learning Extensions (Social Studies, Research Skills)

Have children research medals of honor and what they mean. Draw a picture of one of the medals and write a story about someone who won the medal. Have children discuss age limits on being a soldier and research other countries to find out the age limits they have for military service.

Landau, Elaine. *Veterans Day: Remembering Our War Heroes.* Berkeley Heights, N.J.: Enslow Publishers, 2002. 48p. $23.93. ISBN 0-7660-1775-3.

📖 CHAPTER BOOK—Nonfiction
Ages 8–12

Summary

Color photos supplement this history of Veterans' Day and a description of celebrations and memorials across the country and in schools. Directions for a craft project, a glossary, suggested additional reading, and Web sites for further information complete the book.

Booktalk

(Do not show children the cover of the book before beginning.) It used to be called Armistice Day. It is the anniversary of the end of the World War I. In 1954, the name of the holiday was changed to honor all veterans. A special ceremony is held in Arlington, Virginia, at the Tomb of the Unknown Soldier. Many communities honor veterans with parades. Red paper poppies are the official flower of veterans. The poppies have a special significance. A poem has even been written about them. What is the name of this holiday?

Learning Extensions (Social Studies)

Talk with the children about Veterans' Day celebrations in your own community. Ask them if they have family members, friends, or neighbors who are veterans. Create your own or follow the directions in the back of the book to make a Veterans' Day thank-you card to give to a veteran. Log on to the Web sites listed in the back of the book for more information about Veterans' Day.

White, Ellen Emerson. *The Journal of Patrick Seamus Flaherty: United States Marine Corps.* New York: Scholastic, 2002. 192p. $10.95. ISBN 0-439-14890-1.

📖 CHAPTER BOOK—Fiction
Ages 9–14

Summary

Patrick Seamus Flaherty records in his journal his experiences during the battle of Khe Sanh in Vietnam from December 25, 1967, to April 22, 1968. Like other books in the *Dear America* series, this book ends with an epilogue, a historical note, and photographs. The Military Code of Conduct and the Marines' Hymn are also included.

Booktalk

Smedley, Shadow, and Rotgut; Apollo, Twerp, and Perez. These are the names of Patrick's buddies. Fox, Gunny, and the Professor and Pugsley, Motormouth, Mooch, and Beebop are his buddies too. They call Patrick a lot of names—Boots, Newby, Mick, Boston—until they hit on Mighty Mouse. That is the name that stuck. Who are these men? They're Marines in Vietnam at Khe Sanh. Their platoon was sent to a hill about four miles from the base. Four miles isn't far, but after 76 days, they hadn't gotten back. And not everyone got back.

Learning Extensions (Language Arts)

Encourage children to read Patrick's journal and his sister's diary, *Where Have All the Flowers Gone? The Diary of Molly MacKenzie Flaherty* by Ellen Emerson. Then have them prepare a Readers Theater presentation with students alternately reading excerpts from each book, thereby retelling Patrick's story and the story of his sister and family at home.

Other Books to Use for Veterans' Day

Cotton, Jacqueline S. *Veteran's Day.* New York: Childrens Press, 2002. Ages 4–8. 32p. $5.95. ISBN 0-516-274996.

Henry, Heather French. *Pepper's Purple Heart: A Veterans Day Story.* Woodland Hills, Calif.: Cubbie Blue Publishing, 2004. Ages 4–8. 32p. $15.95. ISBN 0-970-634102.

Myers, Walter Dean. *The Journal of Scott Pendleton Collins: A World War II Soldier.* New York: Scholastic, 1999. Ages 9–12. 140p. $10.95. ISBN 0-439-55503-5.

12.4 THANKSGIVING

In 1863, Abraham Lincoln proclaimed a national Thanksgiving Day to be observed on the fourth Thursday of November. In 1941, Thanksgiving Day became a national public holiday. The Pilgrims celebrated with a harvest feast in 1621 to give thanks for their good harvest. But they were not the first Europeans to celebrate a thanksgiving in North America. Juan Ponce de Leon, Francisco Vasquez de Coronado, and others held thanksgivings in the 1500s.

Anderson, Laurie Halse. *Thank You, Sarah: The Woman Who Saved Thanksgiving.* New York: Simon & Schuster Books for Young Readers, 2002. Unpaged. Illustrated by Matt Faulkner. $16.95. ISBN 0-689-84787-4.

  PICTURE BOOK—Nonfiction
  Ages 5–10

Summary

Sarah Hale, author of "Mary Had A Little Lamb," was a nineteenth-century career woman. She was a mother and a writer. After her husband died, she became America's first woman magazine editor. She also fought to make Thanksgiving a national holiday. A brief history of Thanksgiving, a summary of significant events occurring in 1863, a brief summary of the Civil War, and a biography of Sarah Hale appear at the end of the book.

Booktalk

Who can name a superhero? (Encourage children to call out names.) What makes a superhero? (Encourage responses from the children.) This author says that Sarah Hale was a superhero. Sarah was bold, brave, stubborn, and smart. So what did she do to become a superhero?

Learning Extensions (Language Arts, Social Studies)

Be a superhero! Make a difference! Let your voice be heard! Follow the suggestions at the end of the book by writing to newspaper editors and government representatives, petition community leaders, and lobby Congress.

Eisenberg, Katy Hall, and Lisa Eisenberg. *Turkey Ticklers and Other A-maize-ingly Corny Thanksgiving Knock-Knock Jokes*. New York: HarperFestival, 2000. Unpaged. $6.95. ISBN 0-694-01360-9.

 PICTURE BOOK—Pop-Up Jokes
  Ages 5–8

Summary

Not only is this little pop-up book a collection of Thanksgiving knock-knock jokes, but all the jokes relate to the Thanksgiving play that is the topic of the first joke. To read the punch lines of many of the jokes, open the pop-up flaps.

Read-Aloud

Knock-knock! Who's there? Lift the pop-up flaps to read the Thanksgiving jokes. Read aloud, show the pictures, and open the pop-up flaps.

Learning Extensions (Language Arts)

Share and create more knock-knock jokes. Make a group or class book of knock-knock jokes. Use pop-up flaps in your class book.

Rosen, Michael J. *Thanksgiving Wish.* New York: Blue Sky Press, 1999. Unpaged. Illustrated by John Thompson. $16.95. ISBN 0-590-25563-0.

 PICTURE BOOK—Fiction; Jewish; Asian
 Ages 8–12

Summary

Although this book has colorful, full-page, realistic illustrations, it is not a traditional picture book. The lengthy text sensitively tells the story of a family's first Thanksgiving following the death of the grandmother. The multicultural aspect of a Jewish family and an Asian neighbor is well integrated into the two universal themes of family traditions and of death and the continuation of life.

Booktalk

This is the first Thanksgiving without Grandmother. It is the first Thanksgiving dinner that won't be held at Grandmother's house. All year, Grandmother, whom they called Bubbe, saved every wishbone from every bird she cooked so that each grandchild could make a wish with her. Every year, Bubbe wished the same wish. This year will be different—in more ways than one. And Amanda discovers what Bubba's secret wishbone wish was.

Learning Extensions (Social Studies, Language Arts)

Engage children in a discussion of family traditions, in particular, Thanksgiving practices and wishing on the wishbone, and also a discussion of the experience of death or loss and the continuation of life.

Spirn, Michele Sobel. *The Know-Nothings Talk Turkey.* New York: HarperCollins, 2000. 48p. Illustrated by R. W. Allen. $14.95. ISBN 0-06-028183-9.

 📖 BEGINNING CHAPTER BOOK—Fiction
  Ages 4–8

Summary

This book is a beginning reader with three short chapters about the Know-Nothings: four good friends named Boris, Morris, Doris, and Norris. The Know-Nothings don't know very much, and they tend to be very literal.

Booktalk

If you were a Know-Nothing, what kind of Thanksgiving celebration would you have? Would you get a tree? Exchange gifts? Color eggs? Cut red paper hearts? Boris, Morris, and Norris finally figure out what Thanksgiving is all about—or do they?

Learning Extensions (Language Arts)

Engage children in wordplay using the words with multiple meanings used in the book, such as "serve turkey" and "call." There is enough dialogue in each chapter of this book to prepare and present a Readers Theater retelling. Have children prepare a Readers Theater script with a narrator and the four Know-Nothings: Boris, Morris, Doris, and Norris.

Waters, Kate. *Giving Thanks: The 1621 Harvest Feast.* New York: Scholastic, 2001. 40p. $16.95. ISBN 0-439-24395-5.

 📖 PICTURE BOOK—Fiction
  Ages 6–12

Summary

Color photographs taken at Plimouth Plantation illustrate a re-enactment of what may have happened when the Pilgrims and the Wampanoag people celebrated the first Thanksgiving. Each two-page spread features Dancing Moccasins, a 14-year-old Wampanoag boy, on one page and Resolved, a six-year-old English boy, on the facing page. The reenactment is told through the eyes of the two boys.

Booktalk

You've heard the story of the first Thanksgiving, but what really happened? Come! Let's join Dancing Moccasins, a 14-year-old Wampanoag boy, and Resolved, a six-year-old English boy, at Plimouth Plantation as they enjoy food and games, dancing, and songs. Let's find out what might have really happened on the first Thanksgiving.

Learning Extensions (Social Studies, Critical Thinking, Research Skills)

Use information in the back of the book to differentiate between the myths and the reality of the first Thanksgiving. Note that this book is based on information from a letter that Resolved's stepfather wrote to friends in England. Use information about Thanksgiving traditions among the Wampanoag people and the English colonists as a springboard to a discussion about the practice of giving thanks. Learn more about the history of Thanksgiving as a holiday and food and clothing of the 1620s from information in the back of the book. To learn more about the Wampanoag people and the English colonists, see www.plimoth.org.

Other Books to Use for Thanksgiving

Atwell, Debby. *The Thanksgiving Door.* Boston: Houghton Mifflin, 2003. Ages 6–9. 30p. $15.00. ISBN 0-618-24036-5.

Enderle, Judith Ross, and Stephanie Jacob Gordon. *Hide and Seek Turkeys.* New York: Margaret K. McElderry Books, 2004. Ages 4–8. 32p. Illustrated by Teresa Murfin. $23.95. ISBN 0-689-84715-7.

Rael, Elsa Okon. *Rivka's First Thanksgiving.* New York: Margaret K. McElderry Books, 2001. Ages 5–9. Unpaged. Illustrated by Maryann Kovalski. $6.00. ISBN 0-689-84105-1.

13
December

INTRODUCTION

The anniversary of the bombing of Pearl Harbor by the Japanese in 1941 falls on December 7. Three festive holidays follow: the Jewish celebration of Hanukkah, the Christian celebration of Christmas, and the African-American celebration of Kwanzaa. All three holidays are a time for families to gather and to enjoy special foods and gifts. Selected books lend themselves to responses such as choral reading; Readers Theater; making posters, maps, and PowerPoint presentations; and other activities to develop critical thinking and research skills.

13.1 PEARL HARBOR DAY

Pearl Harbor Day, December 7, is the anniversary of the Japanese attack on the U.S. Navy fleet anchored in Pearl Harbor, Honolulu, Hawaii, in 1941. The United States declared war on Japan in response to the bombing of Pearl Harbor, and the war in the Pacific began.

Anthony, Nathan, and Robert Gardner. *The Bombing of Pearl Harbor in American History.* Berkeley Heights, N.J.: Enslow Publishers, 2001. 104p. $26.60. ISBN 0-7660-1126-7.

 CHAPTER BOOK—Nonfiction
 Ages 10–14

Summary

Eight chapters give an account of the historical events leading up to the bombing of Pearl Harbor, details of the attack, and a summary of the U.S. response and the war in the Pacific. A time line, chapter notes, suggestions for further reading , and Internet addresses complete the book.

Booktalk

There were signs, but the warnings were not heeded. There was the Japanese submarine spotted at the entrance to Pearl Harbor and the submarine that was destroyed. Then there was the blip on the radar screen that indicated oncoming airplanes. Still no one was alarmed. So when the first wave of Japanese planes came, it was a total surprise. The Japanese launched their torpedoes, then fled as the bombers flew in dropping their bombs and dive-bombers fell out of the sky toward their targets. Two hours later, 21 ships and 177 aircraft were either sunk or damaged. More than 3,000 lives were lost and more than 2,000 injured. Why and how did this come to be? What happened next?

Learning Extensions (Social Studies, Research Skills, Language Arts)

This book can be used to launch a unit about the war in the Pacific. Divide your children into eight groups. Let each group choose a chapter to read and report on. Children can use chapter notes, suggestions for further reading, and Internet addresses to research additional information about their topics. Have the children make posters, maps, and PowerPoint presentations and incorporate Readers Theater into their reports.

Duey, Kathleen. *Janey G. Blue: Pearl Harbor, 1941.* New York: Aladdin Paperbacks, 2001. 128p. $4.99. ISBN 0-689-84404-2.

 📖 CHAPTER BOOK—Fiction
   Ages 8–12

Summary

Janey Blue and her family lived in Oahu, Hawaii, on December 7, 1941, when the Japanese bombed Pearl Harbor. This is the story of the families during the first 48 hours following the bombing.

Booktalk

It's Sunday morning. Daddy has left early for Hickam Airfield. Mom is cooking pancakes for Janey and Michael. First they hear planes flying in, then they hear a booming sound, next they feel the ground shake as bombs explode! What is it? Mrs. Fujiwara is running across the yard. Where to go? What to do? Questions begin flooding in. And Daddy—where is he? Is he all right?

Learning Extensions (Language Arts)

Divide the children into two groups. Have one group read *Janey G. Blue: Pearl Harbor, 1941.* Have the other group read *A Boy at War,* described later in this section. Assign roles for Janey and Adam, the two mothers, the two fathers, the younger brother and sister, the Japanese neighbor, and the Japanese housekeeper, Janey's Japanese friend and Adam's Japanese friend. Block the stories and prepare scripts. Have the characters retell the stories by sharing with each other their experiences when the Japanese bombed Pearl Harbor.

Krensy, Stephen. *Pearl Harbor.* New York: Simon & Schuster Books for Young Readers, 2001. 41p. Illustrated by Larry Day. $15.00. ISBN 0-689-84213-9.

📖 **BEGINNING CHAPTER BOOK—Nonfiction**
Ages 7–10

Summary

Five short chapters retell the events of the bombing of Pearl Harbor beginning with a brief account of the war in Europe and the Japanese expansion in Asia, followed by a description of the attack on Pearl Harbor, concluding with a summary of the U.S. entry into the war against Japan and Nazi Germany, which ended in 1945.

Booktalk

Who has heard about Pearl Harbor? Well, you probably heard the story of the Japanese bombing of the U.S. naval ships anchored in the harbor. Did you know that it took only two hours for the Japanese navy to completely destroy the U.S. naval fleet? Why did this happen? How could it happen? And how did our country respond?

Learning Extensions (Social Studies)

A picture of a globe on page 8 shows the sphere of Japanese influence in the Far East and the location of Pearl Harbor in the Hawaiian Islands. Have children use a world map or globe to locate these places. Then, on the same map or globe, have children locate the area of Europe identified on page 7 that had been defeated by Nazi Germany. Finally, locate Great Britain and the United States on the map or globe. Call attention to the size of the free world compared to the size of the world under the domination of Nazi Germany and Japan. Page 39 says, "Thousands swarmed into military recruiting offices to enlist." Ask children why they think so many enlisted in the military.

Mazer, Harry. *A Boy at War.* New York: Aladdin Paperbacks, 2001. 104p. $4.99. ISBN 0-689-84160-4.

📖 **CHAPTER BOOK—Fiction**
Ages 10–14

Summary

Adam's family is a military family stationed in Hawaii. His dad is a naval officer aboard the USS *Arizona* when the Japanese attack.

The story unfolds about Adam and his family during the first hours and first days following the Japanese attack. An author's note provides additional information about the bombing of Pearl Harbor.

Booktalk

Making friends was easy for Adam until his military family moved to Hawaii. Now Adam attends a civilian school with civilian kids. So far, Davi is Adam's only friend. When Adam's dad learns that Davi is Japanese, he reminds Adam that he is a military kid and tells him to choose other friends. When Adam runs into Davi and Martin, they invite him to go fishing with them in Pearl Harbor. Should he go? Adam's dad was called back to his ship, the USS *Arizona,* and he won't be back until later today.

Learning Extensions (Social Studies, Critical Thinking, Research Skills)

Attitudes toward Americans of Japanese ancestry figure prominently in this book. After reading, have the children discuss the following questions: Why did Americans fear and mistrust Americans of Japanese ancestry? What did Americans expect of Americans of Japanese ancestry? How did attitudes and behaviors change after the bombing of Pearl Harbor? Have children research the role of Japanese-Americans in World War II—as soldiers and civilians—and share findings with the group.

Other Books to Use for Pearl Harbor Day

Denenberg, Barry. *Early Sunday Morning: The Pearl Harbor Diary of Amer Billows, Hawaii, 1941.* New York: Scholastic, 2001. Ages 9–14. 160p. $10.95. ISBN 0-439-32874-8.

Sullivan, George. *The Day Pearl Harbor Was Bombed: A Photo History of World War II.* New York: Scholastic, 1991. Ages 8–12. 96p. $5.99. ISBN 0-590-43449-7.

13.2 HANUKKAH

Hanukkah falls in December, beginning on the twenty-fifth day of the Jewish month of Kislev and ending on the second or third day of the Jewish month of Tebet. Hanukkah is an eight-day celebration of the

Maccabees' victory over the Syrians in 165 b.c. Each evening, a candle is lit until all seven candles of the menorah, a seven-branched candelabrum, are lighted. Lighting the candles commemorates the rededication of the Temple by Judas Maccabaeus. The story from the Torah says that there was only enough oil left in the Temple to burn for one day. However, the oil burned for eight days. Families celebrate Hanukkah by lighting the menorah and with special foods, games, and gift giving.

Koss, Amy Goldman. *How I Saved Hanukkah.* New York: Dial Books for Young Readers, 1998. 88p. Illustrated by Diane deGroat. $15.99. ISBN 0-8037-2241-9.

CHAPTER BOOK—Fiction; Jewish
Ages 8–12

Summary

Marla Feinstein and her Jewish family think about Hanukkah, what it commemorates, and the significance of their celebration when Marla's Christian friend, Lucy, spends the holidays with them.

Booktalk

Marla loves the decorations, gifts, and festivities at her friend Lucy's house during the Christmas holidays. The way Marla's family celebrate Hanukkah seems drab and haphazard by comparison. This year, Lucy is spending the holidays with Marla and her family. The girls are excited to be together for five whole days. But Marla is worried! Will Lucy miss the festivities of Christmas with her family? How will she feel and what will she think about the Hanukkah celebration at Marla's house?

Learning Extensions (Critical Thinking Skills)

Have the children compare and contrast the way Lucy's family celebrates Christmas and the way Marla's family celebrates Hanukkah. After discussing and listing the similarities and differences, have the children create collages showing the similarities and differences.

Melmed, Laura Krauss. *Moishe's Miracle.* New York: HarperCollins, 2000. Unpaged. Illustrated by David Slonim. $15.95. ISBN 0-688-14682-1.

  📖 PICTURE BOOK—Fiction; Jewish
  Ages 4–8

Summary

Beginning and ending with a four-line verse, the story of Moishe's magic pan is a variation on the traditional tale "The Magic Pot." Moishe's magic pan makes Hanukkah latkes for Moishe, but only for Moishe. The book ends with a short story telling the origins of Hanukkah.

Booktalk

Hanukkah is about to begin, but Moishe's wife, Baila, doesn't have enough money to buy eggs and flour for latkes. During the night, a stranger leaves a magic pan in the cowshed for Moishe. The magic pan makes latkes for Moishe and changes Baila's life and the fortune of her village forever.

Learning Extensions (Language Arts)

Collect and read other stories about Hanukkah. Set up a display of Hanukkah stories or read and compare variations of the folktale "The Magic Pot" and set up a display of "The Magic Pot" stories, such as *Strega Nona*.

Modesitt, Jeanne. *It's Hanukkah!* New York: Holiday House, 1999. Unpaged. Illustrated by Robin Spowart. $15.95. ISBN 0-8234-1451-5.

  📖 PICTURE BOOK—Poetry; Jewish
  Ages 3–8

Summary

Each two-page spread is a rhyming couplet and soft cartoonlike illustration that tells the story of a mouse family's celebration of Hanukkah. The book ends with a one-page retelling of the Hanukkah story, a description of how the Mouse family lights their menorah, the Hanukah blessings, a latke recipe, and directions for the dreidel game.

Read-Aloud

Read aloud the rhyming couplets. Be sure to show the illustrations. Conclude by reading aloud the Hanukkah story, the description of how the Mouse family lights their menorah, and the Hanukkah blessings.

Learning Extensions (Language Arts)

Make latkes with the children and play the dreidel game, using the directions in the back of the book.

Moss, Marissa. *The Ugly Menorah.* New York: Farrar, Straus & Giroux, 2000. Unpaged. $5.95. ISBN 0-375-48047-8.

 📖 PICTURE BOOK—Fiction; Jewish
  Ages 7–10

Summary

Rachel thought Grandma's menorah was ugly until Grandma told her the story of how Grandpa made it for her when they were first married.

Booktalk

Grandpa died, and now Grandma is alone. Rachel stays with Grandma during Hanukkah to keep her company. Rachel loves the beautiful silver menorah that her family uses. She thinks that Grandma's menorah is ugly. Why, it's nothing more than a wooden board with tin cylinders. Then Grandma tells Rachel the story of how the menorah was made.

Learning Extensions (Language Arts)

Engage children in a discussion of Hanukkah—of what it means and how it is observed. Use the author's note in the beginning of the book that tells the story of Hanukkah with its customary celebrations using the menorah, eating fried foods such as jelly doughnuts and potato pancakes called latkes, playing a gambling game with a dreidel, and exchanging gifts. You might want to serve latkes and play the dreidel game or sing the dreidel song. The traditional Hanukkah blessing is given in Hebrew followed by English toward the end of the book.

Other Books to Use for Hanukkah

Cooper, Alexandra. *Spin the Dreidel!* New York: Little Simon/Nick Jr., 2004. Ages 3–7. 14p. Illustrated by Claudine Gevry. $7.99. ISBN 0-689-86430-2.

Cooper, Ilene. *Sam I Am.* New York: Scholastic, 2004. Ages 9–12. 244p. $15.95. ISBN 0-439-43967-1.

Spinner, Stephanie. *It's a Miracle! A Hanukkah Storybook.* New York: Atheneum Books for Young Readers, 2003. Ages 4–8.Unpaged. Illustrated by Jill McElmurry. $16.96. ISBN 0-689-84493-X.

13.3 CHRISTMAS

Christmas, December 25, celebrates the birth of Christ. The feast originated in Rome during the fourth century. December 25 was the date of a Roman pagan festival, the Saturnalia, celebrating the return of the sun at the winter solstice. From Rome, Christmas was introduced to the East and then spread throughout the world. Churches usually display a crib with figures of the Holy Family, the shepherds, and stable animals. Customs such as merry making, gift giving, and decorating with greenery and lights have their source in the Roman Saturnalia and the Roman New Year. The Teutons added feasting, the Yule log, fir trees, and wassailing. In the United States, Puritans suppressed Christmas celebrations as being pagan in origin. It was not until the middle of the nineteenth century that traditional Christmas celebrations became widespread. Since then, Christmas celebrations have become increasingly commercial and secular.

Ammon, Richard. *An Amish Christmas.* New York: Aladdin Paperbacks, 2000. Unpaged. Illustrated by Pamela Patrick. $5.99. ISBN 0-689-83850-6.

 📖 PICTURE BOOK—Fiction; Amish
  Ages 5–10

Summary

An Amish boy celebrates a rural, Amish Christmas with his family and friends. Realistic, pastel drawings illustrate the text that describes the Christmas Eve school program, Christmas dinner at

Uncle Steve's place, and the Second Day of Christmas at Uncle Amos's place with Grossdawdy and Grossmommy.

Booktalk

Today is Christmas Eve Day. It is the day we have our Christmas program at our school. Tomorrow, after my sister Rachel and I do our chores, we'll open our presents and have breakfast. Then we'll go to Uncle Steve's place for Christmas dinner. After we do chores on the second day of Christmas, we'll hitch up the sleigh and go to Uncle Amos's place, where we'll see Grossdawdy and Grossmommy and play with our cousins. You can come too!

Learning Extensions (Language Arts)

Invite your children to describe their Christmas celebrations. Then use the book as a model and encourage children to write and illustrate their own stories.

Daly, Niki. *What's Cooking, Jamela?* New York: Farrar, Straus & Giroux, 2001. Unpaged. $16.00. ISBN 0-374-35602-5.

 PICTURE BOOK—Fiction; South African
Ages 4–8

Summary

Set in South Africa, this is the story of a little girl whose mother buys a chicken to fatten for Christmas dinner. When Christmas comes, Jamela loses the chicken.

Booktalk

"You can't eat friends!" The ladies in the beauty shop all agreed. Jamela's mother bought a chicken to fatten for their Christmas dinner. Every day, Jamela feeds her chicken, holds her on her lap to feed, and even names her Christmas. Now it's the day before Christmas. What will Jamela do?

Learning Extensions (Language Arts)

Jamela's mother planned to serve chicken, squash, rice, stew, and pudding for Christmas dinner. What do your mothers serve for

Christmas dinner or other December holiday celebrations (for those who don't celebrate Christmas)?

Harrison, Michael, and Christopher Stuart-Clark, eds. *Bright Star Shining: Poems for Christmas.* Grand Rapids, Mich.: Eerdmans Books for Young Readers, 1998. 48p. $15.00. ISBN 0-8028-5177-0.

 📖 PICTURE BOOK—Poetry; Christian
  All Ages

Summary

This collection of Christmas poems by well-known authors such as Boris Pasternak, Kenneth Grahame, Ruth Sawyer, Eleanor Farjeon, Jane Yolen, e. e. cummings, Shel Silverstein, and others is likely to be a welcome addition to the home or school or public library. Poems celebrate religious and secular themes. Children, parents, librarians, and teachers looking for a Christmas poem are likely to find one here.

Read-Aloud

Select a Christmas poem of your choice to read aloud.

Learning Extensions (Language Arts)

Possible responses include choral reading, Readers Theater, acting out, illustrating, or using poems as a model for writing additional poems. Consider using "Carol of he Field Mice" for choral reading, "Christmas Morning" for Readers Theater, or "Country Carol" as a model for writing additional poems.

Jiminez, Francisco. *The Christmas Gift: El regalo de Navidad.* Boston: Houghton Mifflin, 2000. Unpaged. Illustrated by Claire Cotts. $15.00. ISBN 0-395-92869-9.

 📖 PICTURE BOOK—Nonfiction; Mexican-American; Bilingual
  Ages 7–12

Summary

In this bilingual book with English and Spanish text on each page, the author tells a true story from his childhood. As his family was packing to leave the migrant camp to look for work, a young couple tried to sell them a wallet and a handkerchief. Although Papa had no money, Panchito hoped that this Christmas there would be enough to buy him a new red ball. On Christmas morning, there were only bags of candy for Panchito and his brothers. That's why Mama had tears in her eyes until Papa pulled the handkerchief from his pocket for her.

Booktalk

It will soon be Christmas. Panchito's family is moving again. They are migrant workers, and for days they have had no work because of the rain. So they must go to find work. As they prepare to leave the migrant camp, a young couple approaches Papa. They want to sell a wallet or a handkerchief to Papa. Papa says he has no money. No money? Panchito's heart sinks. Panchito wants a ball for Christmas. Panchito has wanted a red ball of his own since he was six years old. Surely, this year there will be enough money for a ball!

Learning Extensions (Language Arts)

Encourage discussion by asking questions. Is there something you had your heart set on? Did you get it? How did you feel? Did you ever not get something that you wanted very badly? How did you feel? Was there something that helped you accept and be happy even though you didn't get your heart's desire?

Other Books to Use for Christmas

Clements, Andrew. *The Last Holiday Concert.* New York: Simon & Schuster Books for Young Readers, 2004. Ages 8–12. 166p. $15.95. ISBN 0-689-84516-2.

Rylant, Cynthia. *Henry and Mudge and a Very Merry Christmas.* New York: Simon & Schuster, 2004. Ages 5–7. 40p. Illustrated by Sucie Stevenson. $14.95. ISBN 0-689-81168-3.

Snow, Alan. *How Santa Really Works.* New York: Atheneum Books for Young Readers, 2004. All ages. $15.95. ISBN 0-689-85817-5.

13.4 KWANZAA

Kwanzaa, which is Swahili for "first fruits," is a seven-day celebration of African heritage. Kwanzaa begins on December 26 and ends on January 1. Special foods, gifts, and the lighting of candles—three red, three green, and one black—play a big part in the celebration. The red candles represent the struggle of African-Americans. The green candles represent hopes and dreams. The black candle represents pride. Children usually receive three gifts: a book, something that represents the past, and a toy. Kwanzaa was first celebrated in 1966. Now it is celebrated in the United States, Canada, England, the Caribbean, and Africa.

Greene, Stephanie (adapted from the script by Lisa D. Hall, Jill Gorey, and Barbara Herndon). *The Rugrats' First Kwanzaa.* New York: Simon Spotlight/Nickelodeon, 2001. Unpaged. Illustrated by Segundo Garcia. $5.99. ISBN 0-689-84191-4.

 PICTURE BOOK—Fiction; African-American
 Ages 4–8

Summary

Susie and her friends celebrate Kwanzaa with Aunt T when she comes to visit on the day after Christmas. The last page explains the holiday of Kwanzaa. Note: In the children's dialogue, the author uses nonstandard spellings and pronunciations such as "Kwonzo," "eggsackly," and "imbentor."

Booktalk

It's Kwanzaa, and Aunt T is coming to visit Susie's family and friends. Aunt T says, "Kwanzaa is about being together as a family to honor our great people!" But Susie doesn't feel great. She hasn't won any awards like other members of her family. She can't help prepare for Kwanzaa. She can't even make a gift for Aunt T. Then Aunt T shows Susie the family album, and Susie discovers that everyone can be great, including herself. What do you suppose Susie finds in the album?

Learning Extensions (Language Arts, Character Education)

Discuss with the children how each of them can be great. Then give each child a piece of paper with the name of another child in the group. Have each child write a note to the other child that says, "(Name), you are great because ..." Have children fold their notes, write the name of the child on the outside, then drop the notes into small box. Select two children: one to draw a note from the box, the other to deliver the note. Finally, invite children to proclaim their greatness by reading their notes: "I am great because ..."

Grier, Ella. *Seven Days of Kwanzaa: A Holiday Step Book.* New York: Viking, 1997. Unpaged. Illustrated by John Ward. $10.99. ISBN 0-670-87327-6.

 PICTURE BOOK—Fiction
Ages 5–10

Summary

Seven pages using a step-book format celebrate Kwanzaa with song, rhyme, music, dance, and foods. Four recipes are included in the back of the book.

Read-Aloud

Read aloud the short text on each page.

Learning Extensions (Language Arts, Music)

Re-read the book, encouraging the children to join in the songs and rhymes. Use the recipe in the back of the book to make Popcorn Nut Crunch.

Related Books

K Is for Kwanzaa: A Kwanzaa Alphabet Book by Juwanda G. Ford and Ken Wilson-Max is a picture book that describes the holiday for the same age-group.

Hamilton, Virginia. *Bluish.* New York: Blue Sky Press, 1999. 128p. $15.95. ISBN 0-590-28879-2.

  📖 CHAPTER BOOK—Fiction; Special Needs; African American; Jewish; Christian
Ages 9–14

Summary

Virginia Hamilton has artfully and authentically woven together the language of the African-American children with the hesitancies and fears surrounding the strangeness of a sick child in a wheelchair. She has also blended the Jewish observance of Hanukkah with the African-American observance of Kwanzaa and the Christian observance of Christmas into a celebration of diversity.

Booktalk

Bluish is what some of the kids call her. That's because of the color of her skin. Bluish sits in a wheelchair. She wears a knitted hat. But little by little, Dreenie and Tulie become friends with Bluish.

Learning Extensions (Character Education, Language Arts)

Consider using this book as a read-aloud and as a basis for exploring and developing attitudes toward diversity. After reading aloud chapter 7, "All of Us," the chapter about Christmas, Hanukkah, and Kwanzaa, create a three-column chart that identifies attributes of Christmas, Hanukkah, and Kwanzaa.

Jones, Amy Robin. *Kwanzaa*. Chanhassen, Minn.: The Child's World, 2001. 40p. ISBN 1-56766-719-8.

  📖 PICTURE BOOK—Fiction; African American
Ages 8–12

Summary

Color photographs supplement the text defining Kwanzaa: its history, the seven principles, and its the celebration. The seven days of Kwanzaa are described, answering questions and suggesting projects and recipes. A glossary, index, list of additional readings, and Web sites complete the book.

Booktalk/Bookwalk

Arrange on a table items such as a cup, a straw basket of fruits and vegetables, and a candle holder with seven candles: one black candle in the center, three red candles to the left of the black candle, and three green candles to the right. Greet the children with the African word of welcome used during Kwanzaa, kukaribisha (koo-kah-ree-BEE-shah). Then translate, telling the children that kukaribisha means welcome. Show the cover of the book and say "welcome to the celebration of Kwanzaa." Then explain that Kwanzaa is observed for seven days beginning on December 26 and ending on January 1. Explain that Kwanzaa is an African-American celebration of family, community, and culture. Call attention to the items on the table and continue to explain that the cup represents unity, the straw basket of fruits and vegetables represents the harvest of collective work, and the candles that are lit, one for each day of the celebration, represent black people, their efforts, and their hopes. Show the book again, turn the pages, and tell children that Kwanzaa was first celebrated in 1966 (pages 6–7), that seven principles provide guidelines for living (pages 10–13), that Kwanzaa is celebrated for seven days (pages 20–25), that there are many ways to make Kwanzaa special (pages 30–33), and that special foods are used during the celebration (pages 34–35).

Learning Extensions (Language Arts, Music, Research Skills)

Plan a Kwanzaa celebration that includes thinking about and honoring the seven principles, lighting the seven candles that are placed in a kinara, reading or retelling African folktales, listening or performing music of African-Americans, and serving traditional foods such as sweet potatoes, plantains, or beans and rice. Use suggestions in the book as a guide. For more information, visit the Web sites listed in the back of the book, such as www.fortunecity.com/victorian/veron/514/15c.html, www.tike.com/celeb-kw.htm, or http://members.aol.com/lindano/Course/pages/kwrecipe.html.

Other Books to Use for Kwanzaa

Chocolate, Deborah. *A Very Special Kwanzaa.* New York: Scholastic, 1996. Ages 7–10. 112p. $3.99. ISBN 0-590-84862-3.

Ford, Juwanda G. *K Is for Kwanzaa: A Kwanzaa Alphabet Book.* New York: Scholastic, 2003. Ages 3–5. 32p. Illustrated by Ken Wilson-Max. $5.99. ISBN 0-439-56071-3.

Medearis, Angela Shelf. *The Seven Days of Kwanzaa.* New York: Scholastic, 1994. Ages 8–12. 112p. $4.50. ISBN 0-590-46360-8.

14
Other Occasions

INTRODUCTION

Other occasions that are cause for celebration are birthdays, loose teeth with visits from the tooth fairy, and the arrival of a new sibling in the family. Raggedy Ann is an old favorite who will delight young readers with her birthday surprise for Raggedy Andy. The story of Blue's birthday is a new favorite based on the *Blue's Clues* television series. Multicultural stories, fantasy, realism, and humor round out the selection of titles for other occasions. Learning Extensions include dramatization, learning, and conversing in Spanish and the development of critical thinking and research skills as well as language arts, science, and social studies activities.

14.1 BIRTHDAYS

Celebrating birthdays is one of the first parties that a child experiences and looks forward to. A birthday is a child's day to be center stage, a time to rejoice in the life of that child. Across time and cultures, a birthday is a celebration of life.

Peters, Stephanie True. *My First Raggedy Ann: Raggedy Ann and the Birthday Surprise.* New York: Simon & Schuster Books for Young Readers, 2000. Unpaged. $15.00. ISBN 0-689-83136-6.

 PICTURE BOOK—Fiction
Ages 3–7

Summary

Raggedy Ann and her friends plan a surprise birthday party for Raggedy Andy.

Booktalk

It's Raggedy Andy's birthday. Raggedy Ann wants to plan a party for him. How will she surprise him? Raggedy Ann has an idea. With the help of Mr. Sparrow, Raggedy Ann prepares an adventure for Raggedy Andy. What do you suppose that adventure might be?

Learning Extensions (Language Arts)

Celebrate Raggedy Andy's birthday by revisiting the text to identify the sequence of events and the characters and prepare a script. Ask children what kind of party they would plan for Raggedy Andy. Make hand puppets to act out the story. Some children may want to create a puppet stage or backdrop as a setting.

Ryan, Pam Munoz. *Mice and Beans.* New York: Scholastic Press, 2001. Unpaged. Illustrated by Joe Cepeda. $15.95. ISBN 0-439-18303-0.

 PICTURE BOOK—Fiction; Hispanic
Ages 7–10

Summary

Rosa Maria prepares a birthday party for her seven-year-old granddaughter, Catalina. She spends the week planning, cleaning, shopping, cooking, and setting mousetraps every night. In the end, Rosa Maria discovers that the mice helped her, so she allows them to live in her house.

Read-Aloud

It is the rhythmic, repetitive language rather than the story line that gives this book its charm. Read and encourage the children to chime in on the repetitive phrases such as "no importa" and the last sentence of each page.

Learning Extensions (Language Arts)

Re-read the book aloud. Turn the pages and show the pictures. Encourage children to read the words in bold print and to repeat the repetitive phrases. Use the glossary and pronunciation guide in the back of the book to learn the Spanish words. Encourage children to use Spanish words they learned when conversing. Extend the book by having a party. Serve enchiladas, rice, and beans like Rosa Maria did. Use the recipe for rice and beans that is on the back cover of the book. Fill a piñata with candy, then string the piñata up so that the children can break it and scramble for the candy. Some children might want to make and decorate their own piñata using papier-mâché and color tissue paper.

Santomero, Angela C. *Blue's Clues: Blue's Big Birthday.* New York: Simon Spotlight, 2002. Unpaged. Illustrated by Traci Paige Johnson and Soo Kyung Kim. $3.50. ISBN 0-689-85103-0.

    PICTURE BOOK—Fiction
    Ages 5–8

Summary

Blue left her paw print on three clues telling the reader what she wants for her birthday. Interactive questions throughout the book invite the reader to look for the clues, help bake a birthday cake, help set the table and put up party decorations, and to match gifts with givers.

Bookwalk

Show the cover of the book, read the title and the author. Tell children that it's Blue's birthday. Show the first two-page spread and tell children that they are going to help get ready for the party. Ask what they think Blue wants for a gift. Show the next two-page spread and tell children that they're going to play Blue's Clues to find out. Ask them to uncover the first clue by blowing away the paw print. Turn the page and identify the first clue (the color green). Turn the page, read aloud, and encourage children to respond. Remind the children to look for clues. Turn the page, read aloud, talk about the second clue (the fish tank), and have children count 10 spoons. Turn the page. Ask children to count the spoons, plates, cups, and napkins on the table and to look for the missing star and missing balloon. Remind them to look for clues. Turn the page and identify the third clue (a shell). Turn the page, talk about the clues, and encourage children to use the clues to guess the gift that Blue wants. Turn the page to find out what Blue wants. Read aloud the last four pages of the book.

Learning Extensions (Critical Thinking Skills)

Ask children to think of something they would like as a birthday gift. Brainstorm possible clues to each gift. Have children make lists of clues for their gifts and then draw pictures that include the clues. Draw paw prints on small sticky notes. Place paw prints over clues. Have children trade pictures, find clues, and guess what the birthday gifts might be.

Stewart, Sarah. *The Journey.* **New York: Farrar, Straus & Giroux, 2001. Unpaged. Illustrated by David Small. $16.00. ISBN 0-374-33905-8.**

  PICTURE BOOK—Fiction; Amish
  Ages 7–12

Summary

Hannah, an Amish girl, travels to Chicago on her birthday with her mother and her mother's friend, Maggie. Hannah writes daily in her diary. Illustrations alternate between Amish life and life in Chicago.

Bookwalk

Introduce the book by showing children the cover; reading the title, author, and illustrator; and telling children that Hannah is an Amish girl who lives on a farm. On her birthday, she visits the city of Chicago for the first time. Engage children in a conversation about what Hannah's life on the farm might be like and what she might see and experience in the city. Then turn the pages and show and talk about the pictures.

The first two-page spread shows Hannah going into a hotel with her mother and her mother's friend Maggie. There are cars and trucks on the street, a sandwich wagon, and newsstands on the sidewalk. Overhead is the elevated train. The next two-page spread shows the view of Chicago and Lake Michigan from Hannah's hotel window. Ask what Hannah might be thinking and writing in her diary. Encourage responses. Continue through the book.

Learning Extensions (Critical Thinking Skills, Language Arts)

Hannah's trip to Chicago made for a memorable birthday. Ask the children what made Hannah's birthday trip memorable. Use the illustrations to compare and contrast Amish life with life in Chicago:: city streets, buildings, and traffic versus houses, barns, fields, gardens, animals, horses, and carriages and manikins and clothing in the department store versus dresses sewn at home. Make a Venn diagram showing what is the same and what is different.

Ask the children to share with the group memorable birthdays they may have had. Stimulate discussion by sharing a memorable birthday that you may have had. Be sure to highlight what made your birthday memorable and ask the children to do the same. Have children write a story about "My Best Birthday Ever"—real or imagined.

Other Books to Use for Birthdays

Cutler, Jane. *The Birthday Doll.* New York: Farrar, Straus & Giroux, 2004. Ages 4–7. Unpaged. $16.00. ISBN 0-374-30719-9.

Look, Lenore. *Henry's First-Moon Birthday.* New York: Atheneum Books for Young Readers. Ages 4–8. Unpaged. Illustrated by Yumi Heo. $16.00. ISBN 0-689-82294-4.

Potter, Giselle. *Chloe's Birthday ... and Me.* New York: Atheneum Books for Young Readers, 2004. Ages 4–8. Unpaged. $15.95. ISBN 0-689-86230-X.

14.2 LOOSE TEETH AND THE TOOTH FAIRY

The legend of the tooth fairy says that when a child loses a tooth, it must be placed under his or her pillow for the tooth fairy. The tooth fairy will come during the night, take the tooth, and leave some money. The legend of the tooth fairy may have its origins with the Vikings who had a tooth fee: a fee given to the child in exchange for the tooth. The child's loose teeth were then strung on a necklace and worn as jewelry. In Europe, children buried their lost teeth. The English practice, dating from the Middle Ages, was for the child to drop the tooth into a fire.

Bourgeois, Paulette, and Brenda Clark. *Franklin and the Tooth Fairy.* New York: Scholastic, 1996. Unpaged. $4.99. ISBN. 0–590–25469–3.

 📖 EASY READER—Fiction
 Ages 5–7

Summary

Franklin's parents buy him a present to celebrate his growing up when he is unhappy he doesn't have teeth to lose and put under his pillow for the tooth fairy.

Booktalk

Franklin's best friend, Bear, loses a tooth and will put it under his pillow for the tooth fairy. Franklin is unhappy because he's a turtle and turtles don't have teeth to lose and put under their pillows for the tooth fairy. How can Franklin be like Bear and his other friends who have teeth?

Learning Extensions (Science, Research Skills)

Have children make a list of animals with teeth and animals with no teeth. Do these animals with teeth fit into a group? How do animals with no teeth chew and digest food? Have children research and report findings.

Klein, Abby. *Tooth Trouble.* New York: Scholastic, 2004. 95p. Illustrated by John McKinley. $3.99. ISBN 0–439–55595–7.

 📖 CHAPTER BOOK—Fiction
  Ages 4–10

Summary

Shark-loving Freddy Thresher is a first grader with a problem. This time he's the only kid in his class who hasn't lost a tooth. Another in the *Get Ready for Freddy* series, this book ends with Freddy's Fun Pages: Freddy's Shark Journal, a fill-in-the-blank story for readers to complete, directions for making a tooth pillow, and a letter from the author inviting readers to write to her. For fun, the illustrator has hidden the word "fin" in the pictures.

Booktalk

Freddy Thresher has a problem. He's the only kid in first grade who hasn't lost a tooth. Then when he does lose his tooth, he swallows it. How will the tooth fairy know to come and leave Freddy some money when he doesn't have a tooth to put under his pillow?

Learning Extensions (Health)

A natural connection for this book is learning about teeth and dental hygiene. Why do children loose their teeth? Why do new teeth grow in? How can we take care of our teeth?

Olson, Mary W. *Nice Try Tooth Fairy.* New York: Simon & Schuster Books for Young Readers, 2000. Unpaged. Illustrated by Katherine Tillotson. $15.00. ISBN 0-689-82422-X.

📖 **PICTURE BOOK**—Fiction
Ages 4–7

Summary

Emma writes a series of letters to the tooth fairy. She lost her first tooth but wants it back to show to her grandfather. The tooth fairy returns the teeth of a rhinoceros, skunk, alligator, and other animals before she finds Emma's tooth. Each animal comes to Emma's bedroom to reclaim its tooth.

Booktalk

Did you ever write a letter to the tooth fairy thanking her for the money she left under your pillow? Emma did. That's how it all started. When Emma's grandfather came to visit, she wrote another letter to the tooth fairy asking for her tooth back to show to her grandfather. The tooth fairy tried. Every night she returned a tooth to Emma—big teeth and small teeth. Every night an animal visited Emma's bedroom to reclaim his tooth—big animals and small animals. Finally, the tooth fairy returned an alligator's tooth. Emma doesn't want an alligator in her bedroom! What will the tooth fairy do? Will she ever find Emma's tooth?

Learning Extensions (Language Arts)

Each two-page spread is a full-color illustration with a letter to the tooth fairy from Emma. Toward the end of the book, a two-page spread with no text shows the tooth fairy searching for Emma's tooth. Show the picture and engage children in an oral discussion about the tooth fairy. How is she feeling? What is she thinking? What might she say to Emma? Then have children write a letter to Emma from the tooth fairy. With young children, use a shared writing approach by writing a group letter dictated by the children. With older children, use a guided writing approach. Make a list of the words and phrases that the tooth fairy might use in her letter to Emma. Then encourage each child to write a letter to the tooth fairy.

Sis, Peter. *Madlenka*. New York: Frances Foster Books, 2000. Unpaged. $17.00. ISBN 0-374-39969-7.

📖 PICTURE BOOK—Fiction; Multicultural
Ages 5–8

Summary

Madlenka lives in New York City. She walks around the block to tell her international neighbors—the French baker, the newspaper man from India, the Italian ice cream truck driver, a German woman, the greengrocer from South America, a classmate from Egypt, and an Asian woman—that her tooth is loose. Richly detailed illustrations supplement the text.

Bookwalk/Read-Aloud

Introduce the book by telling children that Madlenka lives in an apartment in New York and wants to tell her neighbors that her tooth is loose. Begin by showing the cover and introducing Madlenka. Inside the cover, show planet Earth with the tiny red dot, and on the first page show planet Earth, the continent of North America, and the red dot. Turn to the first two-page spread and show New York City: the streets, rivers, bridges, and the red dot. Show the title page and read the title, author, publisher, and place of publication. Talk about the city blocks that are depicted and find Madlenka's block and apartment marked with the red dot. Turn to the next two-page spread, show Madlenka looking out of her window on both pages, and then read-aloud the text. Turn the page and read aloud. Take time to call attention to and talk about Madlenka running from her apartment, down the stairs, and out the door. Turn the page, continue reading, and talk about the pictures. Turn the page, continue reading, and find Mr. Gaston's patisserie in the picture. Turn the page. Encourage children to read the large print and greet Mr. Gaston with Madlenka. Then read Mr. Gaston's greeting to Madlenka. Talk about the picture, call attention to details, and read the text surrounding the picture. Turn the page, call attention to details, and talk about the picture. Turn the page, read the text, and then meet three neighbors who live on Madlenka's block by calling attention to details and reading aloud the text surrounding the picture. (The text surrounding the picture names each neighbor and the country he or she is from.) Then read aloud Mr. Singh's greeting to Madlenka, turn the page, look at the picture, and talk about India. Continue to do the same to the end of the book. Read aloud the last three pages. Look at the picture on the very last page and locate the countries that Madlenka's neighbors came from.

Learning Extensions (Social Studies)

Madlenka told the world that her tooth was loose just by walking around her block. Maybe it was easy for her because New York City is so big and full of all kinds of people. How far do your children have to go to tell the world about their loose teeth? Ask them where their families came from. Find those places on a map. Then ask if they know people who have come from other places: other people in the library, school, or neighborhood or family and friends. Identify other people and places. Find those places on a map. Using the book as a model, name people and the places they came from and add a few pieces of information about each place. Ask children to illustrate their map and information by drawing pictures about people and places.

As a group, decide on a message to send "around the world." Then send it by word of mouth, letters, and e-mail. See what kind of responses you get and how long it takes. Make a chart of where/how the message was sent and if a response was made.

Wilhelm, Hans. *I Lost My Tooth.* New York: Scholastic, 1999. Unpaged. $3.99. ISBN 0-590-64230-8.

 📖 EASY READER—Fiction
   Ages 3–6

Summary

A white, fluffy dog swallows his loose tooth, takes a picture of his mouth with the missing tooth, and places the picture under the pillow in his basket. The tooth fairy takes the picture and leaves treats.

Booktalk

Introduce the book by showing the cover and reading the title, *I Lost My Tooth.* Continue in the first person, still showing the picture of the dog on the cover, and say, :I lost my tooth while I was eating my supper. I think I swallowed my tooth. I wanted to put my tooth under my pillow for the tooth fairy. What will I do now?"

Learning Extensions (Critical Thinking Skills)

Have the children make predictions of what the little dog did. Write a list of the group's predictions. Then have the children read the story to find out what the little dog did. Finally, make a chart and have the children classify their predictions as true or false.

Other Books to Use for Loose Teeth and the Tooth Fairy

MacDonald, Amy. *Cousin Ruth's Tooth.* Boston: Houghton Mifflin, 1996. Ages 4–8. 32p. Illustrated by Marjorie Priceman. $5.95. ISBN 0-618-31099-1.

McMullan Kate. *Fluffy Meets the Tooth Fairy.* New York: Scholastic Readers, 2003. Ages 4–8. 40p. $3.99. ISBN 0-439-12918-4.

Rex, Michael. *The Tooth Fairy.* New York: Cartwheel Books, 2003. Ages 4–6. 32p. $3.99. ISBN 0-439-33490-X.

14.3 NEW SIBLINGS

The arrival of a new sibling into the family is usually a time of major changes. Some new siblings are born into the family, other are adopted. Adoption is an ancient practice of taking children into a family or household. It is mentioned in the Judeo-Christian Bible and dates back to the Greeks, Romans, Egyptians, and Babylonians. The concept of adoption was not recognized in the United States until the 1850s, when the first adoption statutes were passed. Often families in industrialized cities were unable to care for their children, while farm families needed child labor. From 1854 to 1929, children were sent from the cities into rural areas aboard the orphan trains. To protect the privacy of both sets of parents, birth and adoption records were sealed during the 1930s, 1940s, and 1950s. Adopted children had little or no recourse in learning about their birth parents. Since the 1960s and 1970s, some agencies lean toward more open adoptions, while others continue traditional practices.

Browne, Anthony. *Changes.* New York: Farrar, Straus & Giroux, 2002. Unpaged. $6.95. ISBN 0-374-41177-8.

📖 PICTURE BOOK—Fiction
Ages 3–7

Summary

Before Joseph's father left to bring Joseph's mother and the new baby home from the hospital, he told Joseph that things were going to change. While Joseph waits for his father to return, he notices changes, like the teakettle turning into a cat and his slipper turning into a bird. He wonders if these are the changes his father meant.

Read-Aloud

Encourage children to look for changes in the illustrations as you show the pictures and read aloud.

Learning Extensions (Language Arts, Art)

First talk with the children about the changes in the illustrations. Then talk with the children about the changes that occur when a new baby is born into the family. Follow up by having children draw pictures of the changes that occur when a new baby is born into the family.

Bunting, Eve. *Jin Woo.* New York: Clarion Books, 2001. 30p. Illustrated by Chris Soentpiet. $16.00. ISBN 0-395-93872-4.

📖 PICTURE BOOK—Fiction; Korean
Ages 5–9

Summary

Davey is uncertain about the Korean baby his parents are adopting until the baby laughs when Davey plays "this little piggy" with his fingers. The real turning point comes when Davey hangs his rubber duck mobile over the baby's crib.

Booktalk

Davey is hoping the new baby his parents are adopting wouldn't come. By the time Kim Woo's plane landed, Davey's stomach was hurting. The lady said that Kim Woo's name meant Happy Jewel, but names aren't everything, are they?

Learning Extensions (Language Arts, Art)

Davey was worried about a new baby coming into the family until he made the baby laugh playing "this little piggy" with the baby's fingers. After Davey gives his ducks to Kim Woo for Dad to hang over the crib, Davey feels happy again, and he and Kim Woo laugh together. Ask the children if they have ever felt happy when they made someone else happy or when they laughed together with someone else. Have the children share with a partner and then draw a picture of being happy with someone else. Or have children discuss names and their meanings. Children can draw self-portraits that convey the meanings of their names and share with the group.

Cutler, Jane. *Darcy and Gran Don't Like Babies.* New York: Farrar, Straus & Giroux, 2002. Unpaged. Illustrated by Susannah Ryan. $6.95. ISBN 0-374-41686-9.

 PICTURE BOOKS—Fiction
 Ages 5–8

Summary

Darcy didn't like the new baby, and neither did Gran. But Gran helped Darcy change her mind.

Booktalk

Did you ever have a new baby at your house? Did you like the new baby right away? Darcy didn't like the new baby at her house, and neither did Gran. But Gran had a way of helping Darcy change her mind. What do you suppose she did?

Learning Extensions (Language Arts)

Engage children in a conversation about having a new baby at home. Either read aloud or have children read *Darcy and Gran Don't Like Babies.* Then discuss with the children how Gran helped Darcy change her mind.

204 ■ *Other Occasions*

Marx, David F. *Baby in the House.* New York: Childrens Press, 2000. 31p. Illustrated by Cynthia Fisher. $4.95. ISBN 0-516-21688-0.

    📖 EARLY READER—Fiction
       Ages 3–7

Summary

Eve is not happy with a new baby in the house until they have fun together and she learns to love the baby.

Read-Aloud

Show the pictures and read aloud.

Learning Extensions (Language Arts, Art)

After showing the pictures and reading, re-read and encourage children to read along with you. Predictable text and close correspondence between pictures and text will support the children's reading. After re-reading with the children, place the book where the children can easily select it for independent reading. Extend the activity by having the children share their experiences with having a new baby in the house and then draw pictures in sequence to create a storyboard of their experiences. Encourage children who have not had the experience of a new baby in the house to pretend what it might be like.

Mendes, Valerie. *Look at Me, Grandma!* New York: The Chicken House, 2001. Unpaged. Illustrated by Claire Fletcher. $15.95. ISBN 0-439-29654-4.

    📖 PICTURE BOOK—Fiction
       Ages 5–8

Summary

Grandma comes to stay with Jamie while his mother has a new baby. Jamie dreams about Grandma's brother Callum, who died when he was 10 years old. In his dreams, Callum teaches Jamie to ride a bike, swim, and drive the bumper car at the fair. When his mother has his baby sister, Sara, Jamie dreams that he teaches her to ride a bike, swim, and drive the bumper car at the fair.

Booktalk

Jamie misses his mom when she leaves to have the baby. Grandma shows Jamie her picture album and tells him about her big brother, Callum. Now Jamie is going to be a big brother. In his dreams, Jamie discovers what a big brother can be and learns how to be a big brother. What do you suppose Jamie learns about big brothers?

Learning Extensions (Language Arts, Service Learning)

Ask the children if they have big brothers or sisters who helped them learn to do things like ride a bike or swim or if they are big brothers or sisters in their families. Could they teach someone else to ride a bike, to swim, or to do something? Engage children in a conversation about learning from and with each other.

Have children research the organizations Big Brothers and Big Sisters and write mini-essays about them.

Warren, Andrea. *We Rode the Orphan Trains.* Boston: Houghton Mifflin, 2001. 132p. $18.00. ISBN 0-618-11712-1.

    CHAPTER BOOK—Nonfiction
    Ages 10–14

Summary

Here is the story of children who rode the orphan trains to new homes across the country, with photos and commentary from the orphans later in life. Recommended readings, sources used, and information on Web sites and the Orphan Train Heritage Society in Springdale, Arkansas, are given in the back of the book.

Booktalk

Arthur was five years old when he boarded the train in New York City. He and 11 other children rode the train for three days until it reached Clarinda, Iowa. The children were taken to the Methodist church and waited for the crowd of people to look them over. The

Smiths had come only out of curiosity, but then Arthur asked Mr. Smith if he would be his new daddy. Find out about Arthur and other children who rode the orphan trains from 1911 to the 1930s.

Learning Extensions

Learn more about the orphan train riders by accessing Web sites and writing to the Orphan Train Heritage Society at 614 East Emma Avenue, Suite 115, Springdale, Arkansas 72764-4634 (telephone: 501-756-2780; fax: 501-756-0769). Children may also want to research orphans of the nineteenth century (Pony Express riders and lumber camp "cookies" were frequently orphan boys).

Other Books to Use for New Siblings

Cohn, Rachel. *The Steps.* New York: Simon & Schuster Books for Young Readers, 2003. Ages 8–12. 137p. $15.95. ISBN 0-689-84549-9.

Delton, Judy. *Angel's Mother's Baby.* Boston: Houghton Mifflin, 1989, 2003. Ages 8–12. 128p. Illustrated by Jill Weber. $4.95. ISBN 0-618-36919-8.

Hojer, Dan, and Lotta Hojer. *Heart of Mine: A Story of Adoption.* Stockholm: R&S Books, 2001. Ages 4–8. Unpaged. $14.00. ISBN 91-29-65301-0.

Index

Aaseng, Nathan, 157–58
Abenakis, 159
Abraham, 135
Abraham Lincoln (Schmidt), 47–48
Academy of American Poets, 71
Ada, Alma Flor, 125–26
Adams, Abigail, 56
Adams, John, 111
Adoption, 201, 205–6
Afghanistan, 31
Africa, 13, 38, 84, 165, 185
African-American(s). *See also* Kwanzaa; Martin Luther King Jr. Day; National African-American History Month; Slavery
   achievements of, 33, 35
   equal rights to, 23–24
   holidays, 2, 4–5, 33–39
   Kwanzaa and, 2, 4–5
   poetry, 71
   soldiers, 33, 35–36
   in south, 26
African-American Holidays (Winchester), 4–5
A Is for Abigail: An Almanac of American Women (Cheney), 56–57
Alabama, 26

Alaska, 110, 117
Albuquerque, New Mexico, 18
Alcorn, Stephen, 72
Aleutian Islands, 165
Alexander, Sue, 81–82
An Algonquian Year: The Year According to the Full Moon (McCurdy), 158–59
Algonquian Indians, 158–59
All New Crafts for Valentine's Day (Ross), 45–46
All Night, All Day: A Child's First Book of African-American Spirituals (Bryan), 39
Allon, Jeffrey, 14
All Saints' Day, 3, 149–50
All Souls' Day, 3, 149–50
Ambrose, Stephen E., 164–65
America Is (Borden), 112
American Revolution, 111, 112–13
"America the Beautiful" (song), 107
An Amish Christmas (Ammon), 181–82
Amish people, 69, 72, 181–82, 194–95
Ammon, Richard, 181–82
The Ancestors Are Singing (Johnston), 128

Index

Ancona, George, 17–18, 60–61
Anderson, Laurie Hale, 168–69
Angel Face (Weeks), 96–97
Angel's Mother's Baby (Delton), 206
Anning, Mary, 59
Ansary, Mir Tamim, 23, 144–45
Anthony, Nathan, 174–75
Anti-Slavery International, 38
Any Small Goodness: A Novel of the Barrio (Johnston), 126–27
Apalachees, 160
Apple, Margot, 135
Apples and Honey: A Rosh Hashanah Book (Holub), 138
April. *See also* Earth Day; Easter; National Poetry Month; Passover celebrations, 3, 69–84
April Fool's Day, 2
Arabia, 12–13
Are Trees Alive? (Miller), 83–84
Arlington National Cemetery, 164, 167
Armistice Day. *See* Veterans' Day
Ashley Bryan's ABC of African American Poetry (Bryan), 71
Asian, 165
  cultures, 1–2, 84
  festivals/holidays, 5–8
Asian Pacific Heritage Week. *See* National Asian/Pacific Heritage Month
Association for the Study of Afro-American Life and History, 35
Atkins, Jeannine, 55–56
A Tribute to Cajun Music (CD), 61
Atwell, Debby, 172
August celebrations, 117–21. *See also* Back-to-school month
Australia, 3, 95
Aztecs, 94, 148–49

Baby in the House (Marx), 204
Babylonians, 201
Back-to-school month, 117–21

Bahrain, 73
Baishakhi (holiday), 11
Baker, Liza, 95
Balboa, Vasco Nunez de, 35–36
Balfa, Dewey, 61
A Band of Angels (Hopkinson), 36–37
Bangladesh, 11
Banks, Kate, 97, 128–29
Banks, Stephen, 105
Barbour, Karen, 128
Barrios, 123, 127
Bartoletti, Susan Campbell, 102, 129
Bassett, Jeni, 41
Battle of Pueblo (1862), 92, 93
Baumgartner, Ann, 55
Bear Hugs: Romantically Ridiculous Animal Rhymes (Watts and Wilson), 47
Behold the Trees (Alexander and Gore), 81–82
Belgium, 95
Bengali, 11
Bennett, William J., 100–101, 111–12
Bermudez, Diego, 139
Best, Cari, 135
Beto and the Bone Dance (Freschet), 148–49
"Betsy Ross" (book chapter), 100–101
Beyond the Bean Seed: Gardening Activities for Grades K-6, 41
Bhutan, 8, 11
Bible, 79, 201
Birenbaum, Barbara, 39–40
The Birthday Doll (Cutler), 196
Birthdays, 192–96
Births, 4
Bjorkman, Steve, 120–21
Black Hand, White Sails: The Story of African-American Whalers (McKissack and McKissack), 39

Black History Month, 4. *See also* African-American; National African-American History Month
The Black Soldier (Clinton), 35–36
Bloomington, Indiana, 37
Blue's Clues: Blue's Big Birthday (Santomero), 193–94
Bluish (Hamilton), 186–87
Bobrick, Benson, 114
Bogacki, Tomek, 97
The Bombing of Pearl Harbor in American History (Gardner and Anthony), 174–75
Bookwalks, Booktalks, and Read-Alouds (magazine), 17
Borden, Louise A., 50, 112, 114
Boris's Glasses (Cohen and Landstrom), 144
Boston, 63
Bourgeois, Paulette, 84, 196–97
Bowser, Mary Elizabeth, 57–58
Boyajiian, Ann, 58
A Boy at War (Mazer), 176–77
Bradman, Tony, 103
Brahman, 9
Branch, Muriel Miller, 57–58, 106–7
Branch, Willis, 106–7
Brazil, 53, 61. *See also* Carnival
"The Bridge" (poem), 73
Bright Star Shining: Poems for Christmas (Harrison and Stuart-Clark), 183
British Columbia, 110
Brown, Don, 164
Browne, Anthony, 103, 201–2
Browne, Michael Dennis, 104
Bruchac, Joseph, 72, 161
Bryan, Ashley, 39, 71
Buchanan, Yvonne, 107
Buddha, 11
Buddhism, 8, 11, 88
The Bunny Who Found Easter (Zolotow), 81

Bunting, Eve, 202–3
Burleigh, Robert, 129–30
Burma. *See* Myanmar
Bush, George, 157
Byzantine Empire, 13

Cajun(s)
 history of, 61
 music, 54, 61
Cajun Heat Zydeco Band, 61
Calendars
 Gregorian, 16, 22, 27, 66, 74
 Hindu, 66
 Jewish, 16, 74, 135, 177
 lunar, 16, 21–22, 27, 42
California, 37, 55, 157
Calusas, 160
"Calvin Graham: Too Young to Be a Hero?" (Hoose), 165–66
Canada, 40, 109, 185
Canada Day, 109–10
Canada Day (Murphy), 110
O Canada (Harrison), 110
Candlemas Day, 39
Caribbean, 60, 160, 185
Carnival, 2, 53, 59–62
Carnival (Ancona), 60
"Caroline Pickersgill: Stitching the Star-Spangled Banner" (Hoose), 102
Carr, Jan, 44
Carter, Jimmy, 87, 131
Casper Meets Wendy (video), 153
Catalanotto, Peter, 59, 121
Caucasians, 84
Cavender, Bernie, 97
Celebrate Hindu Festivals (Gateshill and Kadodwala), 9–10
Celebrate! In South Asia (Hall and Viesti), 11
Celebrate Islamic Festivals (Knight), 12
Celebrating Chinese New Year (Hoyt-Goldsmith), 44

210 ■ Index

Celebrating Earth Day (McDonnell), 83
Celebrating Passover (Hoyt-Goldsmith), 74–75
Celebrating Ramadan (Hoyt-Goldsmith), 28–29
Celtics, 149, 151
Central Asia, 13, 30
Cepeda, Joe, 192–93
Chancellor, Deborah, 2
Chang and the Bamboo Flute (Hill), 140–41
Changes (Browne), 201–2
Charles, Duke of Orleans, 44
Chatterjee, Debjani, 67
Cheney, Lynne, 51, 56–57
Cherry Blossom Festival, 2, 4
Cherry, Lynne, 40
Chevat, Richie, 77
Child
  labor, 38
  prostitution, 38
Childhood of Famous Americans: Betsy Ross and the Silver Thimble (Greene), 101
Children's Rain Forest, 82–83
The Children's Museum, Boston, 6
China, 3, 12–13, 87, 165
Chinese. *See also* Chinese New Year
  cultures, 2
  Dragon Boat Festival, 5–7
  festivals/holidays, 5–7
  fireworks, 17
  horoscopes, 42–43
  Lantern Festival, 5–7, 42
  Lion Dance, 42
  Mid-Autumn Moon Festival, 5–7
  Qing Ming festival, 5–7
Chinese New Year, 2, 3, 5–6, 34, 42–44
Chloe's Birthday... and Me (Potter), 196
Choral readings, 72–73
Christian. *See also* Easter; *specific holidays*
  celebrations, 59–60, 76, 77–81, 148
  traditions, 29
Christmas, 2, 173
  celebrations, 181–84
  North American, 19–20
  in Philippines, 5
  Spanish, 16–19
Christopher Columbus (Roop and Roop), 146
Christopher Columbus and the Age of Exploration in World History (Sundel), 146
The Christmas Gift: El regalo de Navidad (Jiminez), 183–84
Chronicle of America: American Revolution: 1700-1800 (Masoff), 112–13
Church of Jesus Christ of Latter Day Saints. *See* Mormons
Cinco de Mayo, 19–20, 85, 92–94
Cinco de Mayo (Flanagan), 94
Cinco de Mayo (Vazquez), 93–94
Cinco de Mayo (Wade), 94
Cinco de Mayo: Celebrating Hispanic Pride (Gnojewski), 94
Civil Rights Act of 1964, 23
Civil rights, workers, 21
Civil War, 23, 35–36, 53, 106. *See also* Ellen Bee
Clark, Brenda, 84, 196–97
Clement, Frederic, 87
Clinton, Catherine, 35
Cobb, Jerrie, 55–56
Cochran, Jackie, 55–56
Cockcroft, Jason, 103
Cohen, Peter, 144
Cohn, Rachel, 206
Coil, Suzanne, 60–61
Coleman, Bessie, 55–56
Collins, Eileen, 55–56
Colon, Raul, 126–27
Colorado, 45
Columbus (Ansary), 144–45

Columbus, Christopher, 33, 35–36, 139, 144–46
Columbus Day, 16–19, 139, 144–46
"Come Spring" (poem), 72
Confucianism, 88
Confucius, 85, 87–88
Constitutional Convention, 109
Cooper, Alexandra, 181
Cooper, Floyd, 62
Cooper, Ilene, 13–14, 181
Cooper, Martha, 42
Cortes, Hernando, 35–36
Costa Rica, 16, 18–19, 82–83, 125
Cotton, Jacqueline S., 168
Cousin Ruth's Tooth (MacDonald), 201
Cronin, Doreen, 161
Crunk, Tony, 132
Cultivating a Child's Imagination Through Gardening, 41
Cultures, 2–20, 140. *See also specific cultures*
Curie, Marie, 59
Curry, Jane Louise, 161
Cushman, Doug, 121
Cutler, Jane, 196, 203

Daddy's Lullaby (Bradman), 103
Daddy, Will You Miss Me? (Eachus and McCormick), 105
Daly, Niki, 182–83
Dance, Sing, Remember: A Celebration of Jewish Holidays (Kimmelman), 15
Dancing Wheels (McMahon), 140–41
D'Arc, Karen Scourby, 132–33
Darcy and Gran Don't Like Babies (Cutler), 203
"Dayenu," 75
Day, Larry, 175–76
Day of the Dead, 16–19, 148–59. *See also* Halloween
Day of the Dead (Johnston), 150

The Day Pearl Harbor Was Bombed: A Photo History of World War II (Sullivan), 177
Days of Jubilee (McKissack and McKissack), 107
Days of the Dead (Lasky), 149–50
Deaf Child Crossing (Matlin), 144
Dear America (book series), 167
Dear Ellen Bee: A Civil War Scrapbook of Two Union Spies (Branch and Lyons), 57–58
December celebrations, 173–89
Declaration of Independence, 111
Delaware, 39
Delton, Judy, 206
Denenberg, Barry, 144, 177
Denmark, 95
Desimini, Lisa, 131, 161
Dexter Avenue Baptist Church, 26
El Dia de los Muertos: The Day of the Dead (Wade), 150
Dia de los Muertos, 140. *See also* Day of the Dead
Dickinson, Emily, 56
Disabilities, 139–40, 141–43
Diversity Awareness Month, 140–44
Diviny, Sean, 154
Diwali (Gardeski), 146–47
Diwali, as Festival of Light, 2, 8–10, 140, 146–48
Dobre, Aurelia, 58
Donohue, Dorothy, 44
Doucet, Michael, 61
Douglas, Frederick, 35
Douglass, Susan, 31
Drawson, Blair, 84
A Dream of Freedom: The Civil Rights Movement from 1954 to 1918 (McWhorter), 27
Dr. Pompo's Nose (Elffers and Freymann), 151–52
Duck for President (Cronin), 161–62
Duey, Kathleen, 175
Durbin, William, 130–31

Eachus, Jennifer, 105
Earhart, Amelia, 55–56
Early Sunday Morning: The Pearl Harbor Diary of Amer Billows, Hawaii (Denenberg), 177
Earth Day, 14, 69, 81–84
Easter, 2, 69, 77–81
The Easter Story (Wildsmith), 80–81
East Harlem, New York, 18
"Edna Purtell: Suffragist" (Hoose), 162–63
Education Task Force of Sonoma County (California) Commission on the Status of Women, 55
Egypt, 69, 73, 74, 149, 201
Eid-ul-Fitr (holiday), 11
Eisenberg, Katy Hall, 169
Election Day, 155–56, 161–64
Electoral College, 161
The Elephant-Headed God and Other Hindu Tales (Chatterjee), 67
Elffers, Joost, 151–52
Ellen Bee, 53, 57–58
El Rancho, New Mexico, 18
El Salvador, 125
Elwood and the Witch (Heller), 152
Emancipation Proclamation, 38, 50, 106–7
The Emperor's New Clothes (Demi), 92
Enderle, Judith Ross, 172
England, 94, 109, 111, 115, 185, 196
Erdogan, Buket, 46
Ernest, Lisa Campbell, 105
Esala Perahera procession, 11
Eunice, Louisiana, 61
Europe, 13, 38, 60, 128, 165, 196
Exodus (Wildsmith), 76

Farnsworth, Bill, 49–50, 71
Farris, Christine King, 24–25
Father's Day, 2, 99, 102–6
Faulkner, Matt, 168–69

Feast of All Souls, 148
February. *See also* Chinese New Year; Groundhog Day; National African-American History Month; President's Day; Valentine's Day celebrations, 3, 33–51
Festival of the Bones (San Vicente), 150
Festivals of the World: Costa Rica (Roraff), 18–19
Festivals of the World: Philippines (Mendoza), 6
Fiedler, Joseph Daniel, 126
Fiesta Fireworks (Ancona), 17
Fiesta U.S.A. (Ancona), 17–18
Fight for Freedom: The American Revolutionary War (Bobrick), 114
Finchler, Judy, 118–19
Finland, 95
Fiore, Peter M., 51
Fireflies at Midnight (Singer), 74
The Fire-Maker's Daughter (Pullman), 17
Fireworks
  Chinese, 17
  Spanish, 17
  U.S., 17
"First Saturday Morning: Beaumont, Texas" (poem), 73
Fisher, Cynthia, 204
Fishman, Cathy Goldberg, 135–36
Fisk University, Jubilee Singers at, 33, 36–37
Flag Day, 19–20, 99–102
The Flag Maker (Bartoletti), 102
The Flag of Childhood: Poems from the Middle East (Nye), 73–74
Flaherty, Patrick Seamus, 167–68
Flanagan, Alice K., 94
Fletcher, Claire, 204–5
Florida, 155, 160–61
Fluffy Meets the Groundhog (McMullan), 41

Fluffy Meets the Tooth Fairy (McMullan), 201
Foods
　Indian, 9
　of Philippines, 6
Ford, Juwanda G., 186, 189
Frampton, David, 81
Franklin and the Tooth Fairy (Bourgeois and Clark), 196–97
Franklin, Benjamin, 111
Franklin Plants a Tree (Bourgeois and Clark), 84
"Free at Last" (song), 107
Freedman, Russell, 87
Freedom, Indiana, 33, 37–38
Freeman, Dorothy Rhodes, 63
French, 85, 91, 92–93, 155, 160
Freschet, Gina, 148–49
Freymann, Saxton, 151–52
Fruge, Wade, 61

Gabriel (angel), 27, 29
Ganci, Chris, 131
Gandhi, Mohandas, 23
Ganeri, Anita, 146
Gantos, Jack, 47
Garcia, Segundo, 185–86
Gardeski, Christine Mia, 146–47
Gardner, Robert, 174–75
Garland, Michael, 66
Gaston Goes to Mardi Gras (Rice), 62
Gateshill, Paul, 9
Gender, 140
George-isms (Washington), 50
Germany, 165, 176
Gershon's Monster: A Story for the Jewish New Year (Kimmel), 136–37
Gettysburg Address, 50
Gevry, Claudine, 181
Ghazi, Suhaib Hamid, 27–28
Ghosts of the White House (Harness), 48–49
Gilmour, Rachna, 147

Girls Think of Everything: Stories of Ingenious Inventions by Women (Thimmesh), 59
Girouard, Patrick, 94
Give Her the River: A Father's Wish for His Daughter (Browne), 104–5
Giving Thanks: The 1621 Harvest Feast (Waters), 171–72
Glasser, Robin Preiss, 56
Gnojewski, Carol, 94
Goble, Mary, 109
Gobragh, Erin, 53, 63–64
"Go Down, Moses" (song), 36
Godt, John, 141–42
Goetzl, Robert F., 161
Goldin, Barbara, 14
Gomez, Rebecca, 66
Goodall, Jane, 59
Good Friday, 4, 18
The Good Fight: How World War II Was Won (Ambrose), 164–65
Gordon, Mike, 163
Gordon, Stephanie Jacob, 172
Gore, Leonid, 81–82
Gormley, Beatrice, 59
Graham, Calvin, 165–67
Grandma's Records (Velasquez), 127–28
Grandpa Blows His Penny Whistle Until the Angels Sing (Roth), 134–35
Grandparents' Day, 131–35
Grandpa's Overalls (Crunk), 130
The Great Wave of Kanagawa (Hokusai), 91
Greeks, 38, 85, 94, 132–33, 201
Greene, Stephanie, 101, 185–86
Gregory, Kristiana, 114
Grier, Ella, 186
Grimes, Nikki, 81
Groundhog Day, 34, 39–41
Groundhog Willie's Shadow (Birenbaum), 40
Gryspeerdt, Rebecca, 10

Guatemala, 125
Gulf Wars, 35–36
Gunderson, Mary, 115
Gus and Grandpa at Basketball (Mills), 133–34

Hale, Sarah, 168–69
Hall, Diane, 11
Hallensleben, Georg, 128–29
Hall, Melanie W., 135–36
Halloween, 2, 19, 148–49, 151–54. *See also* Day of the Dead
Halloween Motel (Diviny), 154
Hamilton, Virginia, 186–87
"A Handbook for Young Activists" (book chapter), 82
Hanson, Harriet, 129
Hanukkah, 2, 173, 177–81
Happy, Happy Chinese New Year! (Demi), 44
Harambee, 4. *See also* African-American
Harness, Cheryl, 48–49
Harrison, Benjamin, 144
Harrison, Michael, 183
Harrison, Ted, 110
Hawaii, 174–77
Hayes, Joe, 126
"Healing the Earth" (Hoose), 82–83
Heaney, Marie, 66
Heart of Mine: A Story of Adoption (Hojer and Hojer), 206
Heart People Cards, 45
The Hebrew Months Tell Their Story (Reudor), 16
Hebrews, 69
Heller, Nicholas, 152
Henry, Heather French, 168
Henry, Patrick, 111
Henry's First-Moon Birthday (Look), 196
Heo, Yumi, 196
Hepburn, Katherine, 162

Here Comes Holi: The Festival of Colors (Pandya), 67
Hide and Seek Turkeys (Enderle and Gordon), 172
High, Linda Oatman, 71–72
Hill, Elizabeth Starr, 140–41
Hillenbrand, Will, 65
Hill, Kirkpatrick, 119
Hina Matsuri (Doll Festival), 2
Hindu Festival Tales (Marchant), 10–11
Hinduism, 9, 30–31
Hindus. *See also* Diwali
  beliefs/practices of, 22, 30–31
  calendar, 66
  celebration of Ramnavami, 9
  cultures, 2, 8
  Festival of Bonfires, 8, 10
  festivals/celebrations, 8–11
  year, 9, 146
Hirst, Mike, 9
Hispanic cultures. *See* Latino/Hispanic cultures
Hitty's Travels: Voting Rights Days (Weiss), 163–64
Hojer, Dan, 206
Hojer, Lotta, 206
Hokusai: The Man Who Painted a Mountain (Ray), 91–92
Hold Up the Sky and Other Native American Tales from Texas and the Southern Plains (Curry), 161
Holi, 2, 4, 8–11, 54, 66–67. *See also* Hindus
Holi (Kadodwala), 66–67
Holi (Krishnaswami), 67
Holiday! Celebration Days Around the World (Chancellor), 2–3
Holidays. *See also* specific holidays
  general, 1–20
  origins of, 3–4
  other, 191–206
Holman, Sheri, 88
Holub, Jon, 138

Home to Me: Poems Across America (Hopkins), 72–73
Honduras, 125
Hooray for Mother's Day (Lukes), 97
Hoose, Phillip, 82–83, 102, 114–15, 145–46, 162–63, 165–66
Hopkins, Lee Bennett, 72–73
Hopkinson, Deborah, 36
Horoscopes, 42–43
Hovland, Gary, 51
Howard University, 35
Howe, Julia Ward, 94
How Groundhog's Garden Grew (Cherry), 40–41
How I Celebrate (Robson), 3
How I Saved Hanukkah (Koss), 178
Hoyt-Goldsmith, Diane, 28–29, 44, 61–62, 74–75
A Humble Life: Plain Poems (High), 71–72
Hush, Mama Loves You (Strauss), 96

Id-ul-Fitr. *See also* Ramadan
  meaning of, 27
  observance of, 8–9, 12, 22, 27–31
If the Walls Could Talk: Family Life at the White House (O'Connor), 51
I Live in Tokyo (Takabayashi), 8
I Lost My Tooth (Wilhelm), 200–201
I Love Saturdays y Domingos (Ada), 125–26
I Love You Because You're You (Baker), 95
In Bright Memories (CD), 37
Independence Day, 109, 111–14
Independence Day and Cinco de Mayo (MacMillan), 92–93
Independence Hall, 109
India, 3, 8–13, 31, 38, 165
India (Hirst), 9
Indian(s). *See also specific tribes*
  Algonquian, 158–59
  cultures, 2, 8–11, 39–40, 84
  Delaware, 39

festival of Shivrati, 4
festivals/holidays, 8–11
Florida's, 155, 160–61
Indiana, 33, 37–38, 48
Indigenous Peoples' Day, 144
"In the Great Getting Up Morning" (song), 107
In the Piney Woods (Schotter), 135
Iowa City, 115
Iran, 12–13, 73
Iraq, 73
Ireland, 62–63, 151. *See also* St. Patrick's Day
Islam. *See also* Muslim
  celebrations/festivals, 12–13, 27–31
  cultures OF, 1, 12–13, 30–31
  religion of, 12, 30–31
Islam (Wilkinson), 12–13
Israel, 14, 15, 69–70, 73, 74, 81
Italy, 95
It's A Miracle! A Hanukkah Storybook (Spinner), 181
It's Groundhog Day! (Bassett), 41
It's Hanukkah! (Modesitt), 179–80
It's Our World, Too! Young People Who Are Making a Difference (Hoose), 82
It's St. Patrick's Day! (Gomez), 66

Jahanara: Princess of Princesses, India 1627 (Lasky), 30–31
Janey G. Blue: Pearl Harbor, 1941 (Duey), 175
January. *See also* Id-ul-Fitr; Martin Luther King Jr. Day; Ramadan
  celebrations/holidays, 3, 21–31
Japan, 165, 174–77
Japanese
  Cherry Blossom Festival by, 2, 4
  cultures, 2
  Feast of Lanterns, 8
  festivals/holidays, 5–6, 8
  Hollycock festival by, 2, 4

New Year, 8
Valentine's Day, 8
Jarvis, Ann, 94
Jefferson, Thomas, 111
Jerusalem, 79, 80
At Jerusalem's Gate: Poems of Easter (Grimes), 81
Jesus Christ, 77, 79
Jewish. *See also* Passover; Rosh Hashanah; Yom Kippur
  Arbor Day, 14
  calendar, 16, 74, 135, 177
  cultures, 1–2, 13–16
  Haggadah, 75
  Hanukkah and, 2, 13–15
  holidays, 2, 4, 13–16
  Purim, 4, 13–15
  Shabbat, 13–15
  Shavuot, 13–15
  Simchat Torah, 13–15
  Sukkot, 13–15
  Torah, 178
  traditions, 29
  Tu B'Shevat, 13–15
  Yom Ha'atzma'lit, 15
  Yom Ha-Shoah, 13–15
Jewish Holidays All Year Round (Cooper), 13–14
Jewish Musem, 13–14
"Jewish Storytelling" (book chapter), 14
Jiminez, Francisco, 183–84
Jin Woo (Bunting), 202–3
Johnson, Lyndon, 102–3, 144
Johnson, Tony, 72, 126–27, 128, 150
Johnson, Traci Paige, 193–94
Johnston, Philip, 157
Jones, Amy Robin, 187–99
Jordan, 73
The Journal of Otto Peltonen, a Finnish Immigrant: Hibbing, Minnesota (Durbin), 130–31
Journeys with Florida's Indians (Weitzel), 160–61
The Journal of Patrick Seamus Flaherty: United States Marine Corps (White), 167–68
The Journal of Scott Pendleton Collins (Myers), 168
The Journey (Stewart), 195–97
Juan Verdades: The Man Who Couldn't Tell a Lie (Hayes), 126
Juarez, Benito, 92, 93
Jubilee Singers at Fisk University, 33, 36–37
July celebrations, 109–15
June celebrations, 99–107. *See also* Father's Day; Flag Day; Juneteenth
Juneteenth, 4, 99, 106–7. *See also* African-American
Juneteenth: Freedom Day (Branch), 106–7
Juneteenth Jamboree (Weatherford), 107
Junkanoo, 4–5. *See also* African-American

Kacker, Anisha, 147
Kadodwala, Dilip, 9, 66
Kahn, Katherine J., 138
Katz, Karen, 19–20
Kentucky, 48
Kerven, Rosalind, 29
Key, Francis Scott, 102
Kids on Strike! (Bartoletti), 129
Kimmel, Eric A., 77, 136–37
Kim, Soo Kyung, 193–94
Kindergarten ABC (Rogers), 119–20
King, David C., 115
King, Martin Luther, Jr., 21, 23–27. *See also* Martin Luther King Jr. Day
"A King's Love" (story), 14
K Is for Kwanzaa: A Kwanzaa Alphabet Book (Ford and Wilson-Max), 186, 189
Klein, Abby, 197
Klionda, 40

Knight, Christopher G., 149–50
Knight, Khadijah, 12
The Know-Nothings Talk Turkey (Spirn), 171
Kong Fuzi, 88
Koreans, 88–89, 202–3
Korean War, 35–36
Koss, Amy Goldman, 178
Kovalski, Maryann, 172
Koyukuk river, 117
Krensy, Stephen, 175–76
Krishna, 10
Krishnaswami, Uma, 67
Krudop, Walter Lyon, 89–90
Kung Fu-tzu, 88
Kuwait, 33
Kwanzaa, 2, 4–5, 173, 185–89. *See also* African-American
Kwanzaa (Jones), summary of, 187–88
K-W-L chart (what do we Know, what do we Want to know, and what did we Learn), 85, 93

Labor conditions, 38, 124, 128–31
Labor Day, 19, 128–31
Lady of Ch'iao Kuo Warrior of the South: Southern China. a.d. 531 (Yep), 92
Landau, Elaine, 45, 62, 64–65, 166–67
Landstrom, Olaf, 144
Larranaga, Ana Martin, 152–53
Lasky, Kathryn, 149–50
The Last Snake in Ireland: A Story About St. Patrick (MacGill-Callahan), 65
Latin America, 60
Latino/Hispanic celebrations/festivals/holidays, 16–19, 123, 125–28
Latino/Hispanic cultures, 2, 84, 192–93
Leakey, Mary, 59
Lebanon, 73

The Life and Words of Martin Luther King Jr. (Peck), 27
Lenny and Mel: Holidazed! (Kraft), 20
Lent
  observance of, 21–22, 27, 59, 94
  in Philippines, 5
Leonard, Barbara, 45
Leprechaun Luck: A Wee Book of Irish Wisdom (Gobragh), 63–64
A Lesson for Martin Luther King Jr. (Patrick), 25–26
Levy, Constance, 74
Lew, Elizabeth Van, 57–58
Lewin, Betsy, 161
Lewin, Ted, 50
Libraries Unlimited, Inc., 41
The Life of Peter J. Ganci, a New York City Firefighter (Ganci), 131
Lighting a Lamp: A Diwali Story (Zucker), 148
Lights for Gita (Gilmour), 147
Lincoln, Abraham, 20, 34, 47–50, 93, 168
Lincoln and Me (Borden), 50
Lion Dancer: Ernie Wan's Chinese New Year (Slovenz-Low and Waters), 42–43
Loch Ness Monster, 65
Look at Me, Grandma! (Mendes), 204–5
Look, Lenore, 196
Loomis, Christine, 106
Loose Teeth and the Tooth Fairy, 196–201
Los Angeles, 123, 127
Louisiana, 61
Loveland, Colorado, 45
"Love Letter" (poem), 58
Love One Another: The Story of Easter (Thompson), 79
Lucid, Shannon, 55–56
Lui, Lesley, 140–41
Lukes, Catherine, 97

Lynch, P.J., 66
Lyon, George Ella, 59
Lyons, Mary E., 57–58

MacDonald, Amy, 121, 201
MacGill-Callahan, Sheila, 65
MacMillan, Dianne M., 92–93
Madison, James, 111
Madlenka (Sis), 199–200
Magid Fasts for Ramadan (Matthews), 31
Magnuson, Diana, 83, 101
Mahal, Mumtaz, 30
Mahal, Nur, 30
Malcolm X's Birthday, 4. *See also* African-American
Mama's Coming Home (Banks), 97
Mama Will Be Home Soon (Minchella), 95–96
The Man Who Caught Fish (Krudop), 89–90
Many Nations (Bruchac), 161
March, 20, 53–67. *See also* Carnival; Mardi Gras; National Women's History Month; St. Patrick's Day
Marchant, Kerena, 10
Marcus Garvey's Birthday, 4. *See also* African-American
Marcus, Philip, 129
Mardi Gras, 4, 53, 69–62
Mardi Gras! (Coil), 60–61
Mardi Gras: A Cajun Country Celebration (Hoyt-Goldsmith), 61–62
Mardi Gras — Parades: Music, Parades and Costumes (Landau), 62
On Mardi Gras Day (Shaik), 62
Maria Mitchell: The Soul of an Astronomer (Gormley), 59
Marshall Plan, 165
Martchenko, Michael, 143
Martin Luther King Jr. Day, 21, 23–27
Martin Luther King Jr. Day (Ansary), 23–24

Marx, David F., 75, 137, 204
"Mary Goble: Walking to Zion" (Hoose), 114–15
Mary Margaret's Tree (Drawson), 84
Masoff, Joy, 112–13
Matlin, Marlee, 144
Matthew A.B.C. (Catalanotto), 121
Matthews, Mary, 31
Mauritania, 38
Mayans, 94
May celebrations, 85–97. *See also* Cinco de Mayo; Mother's Day; National Asian/Pacific Heritage Month
Mazer, Harry, 176–77
McCormick, Wendy, 105
McCourt, Lisa, 97
McCurdy, Michael, 158–59
McDonnell, Janet, 83
McElligott, Matthew, 153
McElmurry, Jill, 181
McGee, Dennis, 61
McGill, Alice, 39
McKinley, John, 197
McKissack, Frederick, 39, 107
McKissack, Patricia, 39, 107
McMahon, Patricia, 141–42
McMullan, Kate, 41, 201
McNamara, Margaret, 163
McPhail, David, 95
McQuade, Marion, 131
McWhorter, Diane, 27
Medearis, Angela Shelf, 189
Melmed, Laura Krauss, 178–79
Mendes, Valerie, 204–5
Mendez, Diego, 36
Mendoza, Lunita, 5
Mennonites, 72
Messenger, Messenger (Burleigh), 129–30
Mexican-Americans, 92–93, 183–84. *See also* Cinco de Mayo; Day of the Dead

Mexico, 16, 17, 92–94, 148–50. *See also* Cinco de Mayo; Day of the Dead
Mice and Beans (Ryan), 192–93
Micmacs, 159
Middle East, 69, 73–74
Migdale, Lawrence, 61, 74
Military Code of Conduct, 167
Miller, Debbie S., 83–84
Millman, Issac, 142–43
Mills, Claudia, 133–34
Minchella, Nancy, 95–96
Minnesota, 130–31
Minor, Wendell, 104, 154
Mirror, Mirror on the Wall: The Diary of Bess Brennan, the Perkins School for the Blind (Denenberg), 144
Modesitt, Jeanne, 179–80
Moghul dynasty family tree, 30–31
Mohawks, 40
Moische's Miracle (Melmed), 178–79
Molly Bannaky (McGill), 39
Montgomery, Alabama, 26
Moon, 16
Moonbeams, Dumplings, & Dragon Boats: A Treasury of Chinese Holiday Tales, Activities & Recipes (The Children's Museum, Boston; Simonds; Swartz), 6–7
Moore, Arch, 131
Moore, Cyd, 97
Moore, Harry, 105
Morgantown, Pennsylvania, 39
Mormons, 109, 114–15
Morocco, 73
Morris, James, 39
Morrison, Gordon, 84
Morrison, Lillian, 58
Morris, Robert, 101
Moses, 69, 76
Moss, Marissa, 180
The Most Thankful Thing (McCourt), 97

Mothering Sunday, 94
Mother's Day, 2, 85, 94–97
Mother to Tigers (Lyon), 59
Mouse's First Valentine (Thompson), 46
Muhammad, 12, 13, 27–29
Muhammad (Demi), 31
Munsch, Robert, 143
Murfin, Teresa, 172
Murphy, Patricia J., 110
Muslim(s), 38. *See also* Id-ul-Fitr; Islam; Ramadan
  American, 28–29
  Ashura festival in, 12
  beliefs/practices of, 22, 30
  ceremonies/festivals, 12–13, 27–31, 43
  cultures, 8, 12–13, 27–31
  Hajj festival of, 12
  Hijrah festival of, 12
  Id-ul-Ahha festival of, 12
  Laylat-ul-Barat festival of, 12
  Laylat-ul-Isra wal Mi'raj festival of, 12
  Laylat-ul-Qadr festival of, 12
  Maulid festival of, 12
  year, 21
Muth, Jon J., 136–37
Myanmar (Burma), 11, 165
My Brother Martin: A Sister Remembers Growing Up with Dr. Martin Luther King Jr. (Farris), 24–25
My Dad (Browne), 103–4
Myers, Walter Dean, 168
My First Raggedy Ann: Raggedy Ann and the Birthday Surprise (Peters), 192
My Grandmother Is a Singing Yaya (D'Arc), 132–33
My Name Is Yoon (Recorvits), 92

The Names upon the Harp: Irish Myth and Legend (Heaney), 66
The Name Quilt (Root), 135

Narahashi, Keiko, 95
Nash, Scott, 132
National African-American History Month, 33, 35–39
National American Indian Heritage Month, 155, 157–61
National Arbor Day, 82, 84
National Asian/Pacific Heritage Month, 87–92
National Days, 3
National Poetry Month, 69, 71–74
National Women's History Month, 53–59
Native American Awareness Week, 157
Native Americans, 84, 144, 155, 160–61
Navajo Code Talkers: America's Secret Weapon in World War II (Aaseng), 157–58
Navajos, 155, 157–58
Nawgeentuck, 40
Nebraska, 37, 45
Negro History Week, 35. *See also* National African-American History Month
Nepal, 8, 11, 38
New England colonies, 118
Newfoundland, 110
New Hampshire, 37
Newman, Pauline, 129
New Mexico, 18
New Orleans, 4, 53, 60–62. *See also* Mardi Gras
New Siblings, celebration of, 201–6
New Year. *See also* Rosh Hashanah
  Anglo-Saxon, 151
  of Baisakhi (Sikh), 3
  celebrations for, 2, 3, 11, 19–20
  Chinese, 2, 3, 5–6
  Japanese, 8
  Jewish, 43
  North American, 19–20
  Roman, 181
  Sikh's, 2
New Year's Day, 42
  celebrations, 43
New Year's Eve, 42
New York, 3, 18
New York City, 3, 42, 127–28, 129
Nibbles O'Hare (Paraskevas and Paraskevas), 78
Nicaragua, 125
Nice Try Tooth Fairy (Olson), 197–98
Night Dancer: Mythical Piper of the Native American Southwest (Vaughan), 161
The Night Worker (Banks), 128–29
Nino, Pedro Alonso, 36
Nivola, Claire A., 102
No More Nasty (MacDonald), 121
North American celebrations, 1–2, 19–20, 68. *See also specific holidays*
November celebrations, 3, 155–72. *See also* Election Day; National American Indian Heritage Month; Thanksgiving; Veterans' Day
Nye, Naomi Shihab, 73–74

Oak Tree (Morrison), 84
O'Connor, Jane, 51
October celebrations, 139–54. *See also* Columbus Day; Day of the Dead; Diversity Awareness Month; Diwali; Halloween
Ogden, Betina, 163
Ohri, Kusum, 147
Oklahoma, 37
Olmec, 94
Olson, Mary W., 197
O'Malley, Kevin, 118–19
One Halloween Night (Teague), 153–54
O'Neill, Catherine, 63
Oregon Trail Cooking (Gunderson), 115
Orphan Train Heritage Society, 206

Osborne, Mitchel, 60
Our Country's Founders: A Book of Advice for Young People (Bennett), 100–101, 111–12

Page, Jason, 154
Pakistan, 11, 31, 38
Pak, Soyung, 90–91
Palestine, 73
Palmisciano, Diane, 132–33
Palm Sunday, 4, 80
Pandya, Meenal, 67
Paraskevas, Betty, 78
Paraskevas, Michael, 78
Paris, 60
Parker, Robert Andrew, 114
Paro Tsechu (holiday), 11
A Passover Companion: Wonders and Miracles (Kimmel), 77
The Passover Seder (Sper), 77
Passover, 4, 13–15, 69, 74–77. *See also* Seder
Passover (Marx), 75
Patrick, Denise Lewis, 25–26
Patrick, Pamela, 181–82
Patschke, Steve, 153
Peanuts: Here's to You America! (Schultz), 113–14
Pearl Harbor (Krensy), 175–76
Pearl Harbor Day, 173–77
Pearl's Passover: A Family Celebration Through Stories, Recipes, Crafts, and Songs (Zalben), 77
Peck, Ira, 27
Pennsylvania, 38, 39
Pepper's Purple Heart: A Veterans Day Story (Henry), 168
Peters, Stephanie, 192
Petricic, Dusan, 55
Philippines
 Ati-Atihan holiday in, 5
 Christmas in, 5
 cultures of, 6
 festivals/holidays in, 5–6
 Lent in, 5
 Moriones in, 5
 San Isidro Labrador holiday in, 5
Pick a Dad, Any Dad! (Banks), 105
Pickersgill, Caroline, 99, 102
A Pickles Passover (Chevat), 77
Pilo, Cary, 138
Pioneer Day, 109, 114–15
Pioneer Days: Discover the Past with Fun Projects, Games, Activities, and Recipes (King), 115
Pizzaro, Francisco, 35–36
A Place Called Freedom (Sanders), 37–38
A Place to Grow (Pak), 90–91
Plain People. *See* Mennonite
"Poem" (poem), 73
Poetry, 69, 71–74, 183
Poland, 136, 165
Policeman Lou (Desimini), 131
Potter, Beatrix, 59
Potter, Giselle, 135, 196
Powell, Colin, 35–36
Prange, Beckie, 74
President's Day, 19–20, 34, 47–51
Priceman, Marjorie, 201
Priestley, Alice, 96, 147
Prince Edward Island, 110
Promised Land, 69, 76
Puerto Rico, 127
Pullman, Philip, 17
Pumpkin Heads! (Minor), 154
Punxsutawney, Pennsylvania, 39
Purim, 4
Purtell, Edna, 162–63
Pyrotechnics, 17

Quigley, Sebastian, 154
Qu'ran, 27, 29

Race, 140
Rael, Elsa Okon, 172
Rama, 10
Ramadan. *See also* Id-ul-Fitr

fasting during, 27–28
observance of, 8–9, 12, 21–22, 27–31
Ramadan (Douglass), 31
Ramadan (Ghazi), 27–28
Rau, Dana Meachen, 137–38
Ravi's Diwali Surprise (Kacker), 147
Ray, Deborah Kogan, 91–92
Rayyan, Omar, 27
Readers Theater, 70, 112, 124, 171, 173
Reagan, Ronald, 23
Recorvits, Helen, 92
Reid, Robin, 27
Revolutionary War, 35–36
Rex, Michael, 201
Rhea, 94
Rice, James, 62
Rivka's First Thanksgiving (Rael), 172
Robbins, Ken, 74
Robinet, Harriette Gillem, 26
Robin Hill School: Election Day (McNamara), 163
Robson, Pam, 3
Rocco, Joe, 154
Roman Catholicism, 62–63
Rome, 38, 59–60, 181, 201
Roop, Connie, 146
Roop, Peter, 146
Roosevelt, Franklin, 144
Root, Barry, 129–30
Root, Kimberly Bulcken, 135
Root, Phyllis, 135
Roraff, Susan, 18–19
Rosen, Michael J., 170
Rosh Hashanah, 13–15, 43, 135–38
Rosh Hashanah and Yom Kippur (Marx), 137
Rosh Hashanah and Yom Kippur (Rau), 137–38
On Rosh Hashanah and Yom Kippur (Fishman), 135–36
Ross, Betsy, 93, 99, 100–101
Ross, Colonel, 101

Ross, Kathy, 45
Roth, Susan L., 134–35
Rotten Ralph's Rotten Romance (Gantos), 47
Rouss, Sylvia, 138
Royal Diaries, 88
Rubin, Joel, 82
The Rugrats' First Kwanzaa (Greene), 185–86
Rush, Benjamin, 111
Ryan, Pam Munoz, 192–93
Ryan, Susannah, 203

Saint Patrick (Tompert), 66
St. Patrick's Day, 20, 53, 62–66
St. Patrick's Day (Freeman), 63
St. Valentine, 2, 44
Saint Valentine (Tompert), 37
Salt Lake City, Utah, 109, 114–15
Sam I Am (Cooper), 181
Sammy Spider's First Rosh Hashanah (Rouss), 138
Samuel, Catherine, 81
Sanders, Scott Russell, 37
San Francisco, 18
Santomero, Angela C., 193–94
San Vicente, Luis, 150
Saturnalia, 59–60, 181
Saudi Arabia, 73
Saunders, Zina, 81
Savadier, Elivia, 125–26
Saxons, 77
Schaefer, Lola M., 93
Schmidt, Suzy, 47–48
Schotter, Roni, 135
Schuett, Stacey, 83–84
Schultz, Charles M., 113–14
Scotland, 3, 65
Scott, Blanche Stuart, 55
Secret of the Stone (Taylor), 159–60
Seder, 74–77. *See also* Passover
Segregation laws, 23

September celebrations, 3, 123–38.
  See also Grandparents' Day; Labor Day; Rosh Hashanah
The Seven Days of Kwanzaa (Medearis), 189
Seven Days of Kwanzaa: A Holiday Step Book (Grier), 186
Sexual preferences, 140
Shah Jahan, 30
Shaik, Fatima, 62
Shamanism, 88
Shephard, Ellen, 36–37
"Shivery Winter Mornings" (poem), 72
Sidman, Joyce, 74
Sikh
  celebration of Guru Nanak's birthday, 8–9
  celebrations, 2, 3
  cultures, 9
  New Year of Baisakhi, 3
Simonds, Nina, 6
Singer, Marilyn, 74
Sis, Peter, 198–99
Slavery, 33, 38, 99
Slavery: Bondage Throughout History (Watkins), 38
Sleds on Boston Common (Borden), 114
Slonim, David, 178–79
Slovenz-Low, Madeline, 42
Small, David, 194–95
Smith, Cat Bowman, 121
Smith, Joseph A., 152
Smith, Ken, 62
Soentpiet, Chris, 24, 202–3
Soman, David, 74
Sondak: Princess of the Moon and Stars (Holman), 88–89
Sondak, Queen, 88–89
Song of the Water Boatman (Sidman), 74
South Asia, 8
Southeast Asia, 12–13, 38
Spain, 12–13
Spanish, 191. *See also* Cinco de Mayo; Day of the Dead
  celebrations/fiestas/holidays, 16–19, 148–50
  Christmas, 16–19
  cultures, 1, 16–19, 125
  explorers, 35, 155, 160
  Harlem, 123, 127–28
  Holy Week, 16–19
  Judas Day, 18
  Oxcart Driver's Day, 16–19
  Three Kings' Day, 16–19
  Virgin of the Angels, 16–19
Spanish-American War, 35–36
Sper, Emily, 77
Spinner, Stephanie, 181
Spin the Driedel! (Cooper), 181
Spirn, Michele Sobel, 171
Splash! Poems of Our Watery World (Levy), 74
The Spooky Book (Patschke), 153
Spowart, Robin, 179–80
Spring, celebrations/festivals, 4, 42
Sri Lanka, 8, 11
"The Star-Spangled Banner" (song), 102, 107
The Steps (Cohn), 206
Stewart, Sarah, 194–95
Stock, Catherine, 133–34
The Story of Columbus (Ganeri), 146
St. Patrick's Day, 2
Strauss, Anna, 96
Stuart-Clark, Christopher, 183
Sudan, 38
Suffragists, 162–63
Sullivan, George, 177
Sumeria, 33, 38
Sun, 16
Sundel, Al, 146
Swahili, 185
Swartz, Leslie, 6
Sweet Hearts (Carr), 44
Sweet, Melissa, 58, 59

Swiatkowska, Gabi, 92
"Swing Low, Sweet Chariot" (song), 36
Sydney, Australia, 3
Syria, 73

Taj Mahal, 30
Takabayashi, Mari, 8
A Tale for Easter (Tudor), 79–80
"Talk" (poem), 73
Tangerines, 3
Taylor, Harriet Peek, 159–60
Teague, Mark, 153–54
The Ten Best Things About My Dad (Loomis), 106
Ten Holiday Jewish Children's Stories (Goldin), 14–15
Tennessee, 37, 38
Testing Miss Malarkey (Finchler), 118–19
The Test (Instructional Performance Through Understanding), 118–19
Texas, 99, 106
Thanksgiving, 19, 155–56, 168–72
"Thanksgiving Dinner" (poem), 72
Thanksgiving Wish (Rosen), 170
The Thanksgiving Door (Atwell), 172
Thank You, Dr. King! (Reid), 27
Thank You, Sarah: The Woman Who Saved Thanksgiving (Anderson), 168–69
That Is the Van That Dad Cleaned (Ernest), 105
The Sky's the Limit: Stories of Discovery by Women and Girls (Thimmesh), 58–59
Thimmesh, Catherine, 58–59
This Next New Year (Wong), 43
Thompson, John, 170
Thompson, Lauren, 46, 79
"'Tierra!' When Two Worlds Met" (Hoose), 145–46
Tihar (holiday), 11
Tillotson, Katherine, 197
Times Square, 3

Timetables of History: A Horizontal Linkage of People and Events, 89
Timmy's Eggs-Ray Vision (Samuel), 81
Timucuas, 160
Tomb of the Unknown Soldier, 164, 167
Tompert, Ann, 37, 66
The Tooth Fairy (Rex), 201
Tooth Trouble (Klein), 197
The Trucker (Weatherby), 131
Truong, Marcelino, 90
Tudor, Tasha, 79–80
Tultepec, Mexico, 17
Tunisia, 73
Turkey, 95
Turkey Ticklers and Other A-maizeingly Corny Thanksgiving Knock-Knock Jokes (Eisenberg), 169–70
The Tuskegee Airmen (video), 36
Twelve Hats for Lena: A Book of Months (Katz), 19–20

The Ugly Menorah (Moss), 180
United Nations' Declaration of Human Rights, 38
United States, 16, 92, 94–95, 109–10, 185. *See also* Election Day; Independence Day; other holidays; President's Day; Veterans' Day
 fireworks in, 17
 people in, 33–34, 69
 public schooling in, 118–19
 slavery in, 38
U.S. Bill of Rights, 38, 111
U.S. Congress, 163
U.S. Constitution, 111, 164
U.S. Marine Corps, 157–58, 167–68
U.S. Navy, 174–77
USS *Arizona*, 176–77
Utah, 109

Vail, Rachel, 120–21
Valentine, Nebraska, 45
Valentine's Day, 2, 34

celebration of, 44–47
Japanese, 8
North American, 19–20
Valentine's Day: Candy, Love, and Hearts (Landau), 45
Van Steenwyk, Elizabeth, 49–50
Vargus, Nancy Reginelli, 94
Vaughan, Marcia, 161
Vazques, Sarah, 93–94
Velasquez, Eric, 127–28
Veterans' Day, 155–56, 164–68
Veterans' Day (Cotton), 168
Veterans Day: Remembering Our War Heroes (Landau), 166–67
Viesti, Joe, 11
Vietnam, 2–3, 156
Vietnam War, 2–3, 35–36, 167
Vikings, 196
A Voice from the Wilderness: The Story of Anna Howard Shaw (Brown), 164

Wabash River, 37
Wade, Mary Dodson, 94, 150
"Wake Up and Beat the Drums" (story), 14
Walking to the Bus-Rider Blues (Robinet), 26
Wampanoags, 159
Ward, John, 186
War of 1812, 102
Warren, Andrea, 205–6
Washington, George, 20, 47, 49, 50, 93, 100–101, 109, 111
Washington's Birthday. *See* President's Day
Waters, Kate, 42, 171–72
Watkins, Richard, 38
Watts, James, 161
Watts, Suzanne, 47
We Are Patriots: Hope's Revolutionary War Diary (Gregory), 114
Weatherby, Brenda, 131
Weatherby, Mark, 131
Weatherford, Carole Boston, 107

Weber, Jill, 206
Webster, Noah, 111
Weddings, 4
Weeks, Sarah, 96–97
Weiss, Ellen, 163
Weitzel, Kelley G., 160
We Rode the Orphan Trains (Warren), 205–6
West Virginia, 131
We Were There, Too! Young People in U.S. History (Hoose), 102, 114–15, 145–46, 162–63, 165–66
Whamboozle (Page), 154
What's Cooking, Jamela? (Daly), 182–83
What Teachers Can't Do (Wood), 121
When Abraham Talked to the Trees (Van Steenwyk), 49–50
*When Catherine the Great and I Were Eigh*t (Best), 135
When Washington Crossed the Delaware: A Wintertime Story for Young Patriots (Cheney), 51
Where Have All the Flowers Gone? The Diary of Molly MacKenzie Flaherty (White), 167–68
White, Ellen Emerson, 167–68
White House, 164
Why Do We Celebrate That? (Wilcox), 3–4
Wilcox, Jane, 3–4
Wildsmith, Brian, 76, 80–81
"Wildwood By-the-Sea" (poem), 73
Wilhelm, Hans, 200–201
Wilkinson, Philip, 12–13
Wilson, Karma, 47
Wilson-Max, Ken, 186, 189
Wilson, Woodrow, 94, 100
Winchester, Faith, 4–5
Wings and Rockets: The Story of Women in Air and Space (Atkins), 55–56
Winter, Jeanette, 150
Wisconsin, 38
Wong, Janet S., 43

Wood, Douglas, 121
Woodson, Carter G., 35
Woo! The Not-So-Scary Ghost (Larranaga), 152–53
The World Before This One (Martin), 158
World War I, 35–36, 166
World War II, 35–36, 157–58, 165. *See also* Pearl Harbor Day
Wright, Katherine, 55

The Year of Miss Agnes (Hill), 119
Yemen, 73
Yep, Lawrence, 92
Yolen, Jane, 72

Yom Kippur, 13–14, 22, 27, 135–38
"You Can Be Like Martin: A Tribute to Dr. Martin Luther King Jr.," 25
Young, Brigham, 109, 114
Young, Eliza, 102
Young, Mary, 102

Zaharias, Babe, 58
Zalben, Jane Bresken, 76–77
Zion. *See* Salt Lake City, Utah
Zodiac, 16
Zolotow, Charlotte, 81
Zoom! (Munsch), 143
Zucker, Jonny, 148

About the Author

ROSANNE J. BLASS is former professor of education, University of South Florida, and author, and workshop presenter based in Clearwater, Florida.